PRENTICE-HALL FOUNDATIONS OF FINANCE SERIES

PRENTICE-HALL FOUNDATIONS OF FINANCE SERIES

Ezra Solomon, *Editor*

The Scope
and Methodology of Finance

J. Fred Weston

Chairman, Finance Department
University of California

PRENTICE-HALL, INC., Englewood Cliffs, New Jersey

Library of Congress Catalog Card No. 66-19883
Printed in the United States of America [79656-C]

Current printing (last digit):
10   9   8   7   6   5   4   3   2   1

PRENTICE-HALL INTERNATIONAL, INC., *London*
PRENTICE-HALL OF AUSTRALIA, PTY. LTD., *Sydney*
PRENTICE-HALL OF CANADA, LTD., *Toronto*
PRENTICE-HALL OF INDIA (PRIVATE) LTD., *New Delhi*
PRENTICE-HALL OF JAPAN, INC., *Tokyo*

Editor's Note

The subject matter of Financial Management is in the process of rapid change. A growing analytical content, virtually nonexistent ten years ago, has displaced the earlier descriptive treatment as the center of emphasis in the field.

These developments have created problems both for teachers and students. On the one hand, recent and current thinking, which is addressed to basic questions that cut across traditional divisions of the subject matter, do not fit neatly into the older structure of academic courses and texts in Corporate Finance. On the other hand, the new developments have not yet stabilized and as a result have not yet reached the degree of certainty, lucidity, and freedom from controversy that would permit all of them to be captured within a single, straightforward treatment at the textbook level. Indeed, given the present rate of change, it will be years before such a development can be expected.

One solution to the problem, which the present Foundations of Finance Series tries to provide, is to cover the major components of the subject through short independent studies. These individual essays provide a vehicle through which the writer can concentrate on a single sequence of ideas, and thus communicate some of the excitement of current thinking and controversy. For the teacher and student, the separate self-contained books provide a flexible up-to-date survey of current on each sub-area covered, and at the same time permit maximum flexibility in course and curriculum design.

EZRA SOLOMON

Preface

The field of Finance has undergone a great transformation in recent years. From a body of materials describing instruments and institutions, the subject matter of finance is developing into a body of analytical methods. The emerging focus of finance goes beyond traditional preoccupation with the procurement of funds to analysis of their effective utilization as a part of the general management of the firm to maximize the value of the firm.

These changes have resulted from a number of forces and streams of influence. Significant developments in the external environment and in the tools of analysis have had major impacts on the finance field.

The major changes in the external environment have been many. Five will be enumerated. (1) The pace of technological change has increased, shortening the life cycle of individual products. (2) The pressure on profit margins overall and particularly in industries subject to the competition of new product developments has increased competitive pressures in the American economy. The penalties of being "second-best" have increased. (3) The sustained period of economic growth following World War II has increased the rewards of anticipating new opportunities and making provision for the financial means to participate in growth. (4) The continued development of large scale enterprise has resulted in firms too large to be administered by one man and has required the decentralization of a number of activities. This decentralization has increased the need for planning and control methods to maximize the contribution of individual departments to the overall performance of the enterprise. (5) The institutionalization of the flow of savings and investment has resulted in the professionalization of the investment of funds. This has stimulated analytical methods for evaluating firms and this increased sophistication in turn has led to an expectation that the firms in which investments are made demonstrate that the funds will be utilized effectively.

At the same time that fundamental changes were taking place in the external environment, the tools of analysis have been developing. Model mathematical models sharpened the recognition of the nature of theoretical systems. Management science emerged to utilize teams with competence in basic sciences as well as knowledge of the fields of application. The computer permits large scale processing of masses of data. The programming of the computer requires that the problems be expressed in an analytical form. The ability to process large masses of information with the computer has tended to break down the boundaries of the individual business management functions and activities of the firm to combine them in taking an overall systems approach to the processes of the firm's activity.

The trends in the environment and the increased power of the tools of analysis have had substantial impacts on economic theory and business subjects related to the theory of the firm. The preoccupation of the theory of the firm with profit maximization in the short run was jarred by recognition of the heightening of the tempo of technological change. Shortened product cycles and the impact of new product competition as well as competition in traditional product lines increased the importance of capital investment planning by the firm. Capital theory and financial planning began to be inextricably intertwined with the central issues of the theory of the firm.

With the awareness of the increased pace of change, the major problem of uncertainty again came to be recognized as a central factor in the valuation of the firm. Uncertainty makes it necessary for a firm to develop a strategy for benefiting from opportunities and protection against adverse change. Strategies involve both the optimal mix of asset investments as well as the optimal mix of financing.

The increased sophistication of economic theory has also carried over into the field of finance. The powers of investigation have been greatly enhanced by the new tools of analysis. But the increased facility for building models, the plethora of data and the computer for processing problems also carry dangers. A great increase in the flow of research output is inevitable. But we are in danger of becoming overwhelmed by the volume of output. It may become increasingly impossible to digest the output reflecting rival theories.

Three major differences may result in research outputs that are in disagreement. First, the research may start with different models based on differing basic assumptions upon which the models are developed. Second, the same model may be tested with measurement procedures which employ different variables or measure the same variable differently. An example of the latter should provide a convincing illustration. One of the factors generally regarded as being important for influencing the value of the firm is its rate of growth. Growth may be measured in a number of ways: (1) by total assets, (2) by fixed assets only, (3) by sales, (4) by total net income, (5) by income per share, (6) by the amount of retained earnings, (7) by the ratio of retained earnings to earnings per share, and so forth. The measurement may be over the previous year or estimates for future years may be attempted. The duration of the estimate may vary from 3 years or less to 10 years or more. Some give greater weight to the most recent years. Empirical results may be sensitive to how the variable is measured.

A third area of a major difference in measurement procedures is the use of cross sections vs. time series analysis. The cross section analysis may employ industries, or firms within industries, or samples of firms over a number of industries. The selection of data may emphasize homogeneity or randomness.

The foregoing represent only a sample of the possible variations. It is readily apparent that we are in danger of being overwhelmed by the sheer volume of output in disagreement. The need for reflection and responsibility in our selection of research methodologies has become more important than it has ever been. The need for discipline in use of methodologies is heightened.

The mission of the present monograph is to contribute to awareness of the importance of the influence of methodology on results. The aim of the monograph is to improve methodology in research on finance. The monograph is addressed to the finance field because of its increased significance for the theory of the firm and its critical role in theories of the processes and growth of the economic system as a whole. The focus is on the financial manager and his functions because of the major transformations that have been taking place in his role.

The nature of the financial manager's role in modern business enterprise has interested me since my survey and studies performed in 1953. The methodology of the finance field was an area of central concern in my 1955 paper on theories in business finance. Thus the subject matter of this monograph has been an area of direct interest to me for over a decade.

The present manuscript owes its existence to three influences. The first was a number of discussions with Professor Ezra Solomon in the summer of 1963 on the need for a systematic review of the literature and a formulation of some basic themes, relating finance to both the economic and behavioral theories of the firm. The second was the intellectual ferment stirred by a series of analytical treatments of the finance field beginning with the articles on the cost of capital by Professors Franco Modigliani and Merton Miller.

The third influence was the stimulation received from a series of field interviews in connection with another study. I wish to record my great appreciation to the McKinsey Foundation for Management Research in connection with the completion of this manuscript. I had been struggling for years to complete a follow-up to my article of 1954 in the *Journal of Finance* on the "Finance Function." I was unable to resolve the wide range of overlapping and conflicting threads. However, during 1964 and 1965, I conducted a series of field interviews with the financial officers of a number of firms, large and small, under a grant from the McKinsey Foundation. The discussions were mainly on corporate resource allocation, with special emphasis on financial planning and control policies. As a result of these discussions, the subject of the present study began to fall into a logical pattern which I have sought to convey in the pages that follow.

Helpful comments from my colleagues at UCLA and from Professors H. Igor Ansoff and Allan H. Meltzer of the Carnegie Institute of Technology are gratefully acknowledged.

J. Fred Weston

Table of Contents

The Scope
and Methodology of Finance

The Fundamental Issues of Delineating the Finance Function

THE SCOPE and content of the finance field have been matters of serious inquiry for more than two decades. In the early 1940's, the traditional emphasis of business finance was challenged in a penetrating article by Professor Pearson Hunt.[1] A number of significant issues were raised which stimulated a series of discussions and writings that have continued to the present. During this period of reexamination, the studies in finance exhibited important new directions and dimensions, new significance and increased sophistication. At the same time, the importance of the finance function in the management of economic resources appeared to increase.[2] The significant issues, however, have not been resolved, and there is no clear convergence of academic opinion and professional practice on the proper subject of the finance field.

By a review of methodology, this book seeks to provide a foundation and framework for a better understanding of the nature of the finance function. In this chapter, the fundamental issues are set out, and the nature of the different points of view are explained. An

---

[1] Pearson Hunt, "Financial Policy of Corporations," *Quarterly Journal of Economics*, LVII (February, 1943), 303-13.

[2] "The New Power of the Financial Executives," *Fortune*, LXV (January, 1962), 81-85, 138, 143.

analysis of the scope, orientation, goals, concepts, and tools of finance is also included.

Chapter 2 provides perspective by tracing the evolution of the finance function. A series of time periods since the turn of the century are identified and related to important economic and industrial developments. These are discussed in relationship to the impact on the content of finance studies. Chapter 3 analyzes methodological issues. Every subject must consider such issues if a clear understanding of the field is to be had. Here, the behavioral theory of the firm is contrasted with the economic theory of the firm, and it will be shown that finance thought and practice include characteristics from both theoretical approaches. Chapter 4 examines the finance function in the framework of neo-classical organization and management theory. It includes a discussion of the place of finance in the general management framework of the operation of the firm and indicates the relationship between generic management functions and the specific finance functions. The role of financial executives at both the corporate and division levels is discussed as well. Chapter 5 discusses the financial policies of business firms. While business policies of all types are generally treated in writings on management theory, surprisingly little attention is given to formulating the issues of financial policy.

The materials of the first five chapters provide a background for developing a clear delineation of the finance function in Chapter 6. Here, the major environmental developments which have produced the evolution of the finance function are reviewed, the implications of these emerging trends for the future are discussed, and the important financial decision areas are identified. In Chapter 7, the implications of financial decisions on economic behavior are analyzed. Chapter 8 sets forth the impact of new developments in financial theory on economic theory.

By an analysis of the environment, the nature of modern corporate management, and by a consideration of new tools of analysis, the nature of the finance function will be more clearly understood. Although all the issues may not be resolved, a better understanding will be developed. Let us turn, then, to a discussion of the fundamental issues.

The Scope of the Finance Function

Theories vs. Policies

In discussions on the proper scope of the finance field, some writers have emphasized the development of a foundation of theory, while others have emphasized the recognition of sound financial policy. In a conference on the development of theory in finance, one of the discussants felt that the difference between theory and policy had not been made clear.

> Similarly, I am convinced that we need to clarify our conception of a *theory* of business finance. In Professor Dauten's paper, I feel the concept is closely linked to that of managerial financial *policy;* in Professor Weston's presentation, I find it identified rather with the scientific validation of propositions. Hence the question: what do we mean by *theory,* and wherein, if at all, is it to be differentiated from *policy?* (Italics his.) [3]

While this distinction is analyzed more completely in the chapter on methodology, a preliminary differentiation may be made. Theories specify relations between events. Policies represent decision rules. Policies, therefore, are based on theories.

Despite considerable attention to the subject matter of finance, there is a lack of well-defined theory in the finance field, and there is no agreement on the scope and range to be encompassed by theory. This is also pointed out clearly by Professor Dauten.

> To an outsider it may appear to be incongruous that the present status of the field of business finance is such that there should be discussion of the ingredients of a theory in the field. In most established fields of knowledge there is some disagreement especially about peripheral areas, but a core of knowledge has been developed into generally accepted generalizations or theories in the field. [4]

In my judgment the foregoing quotation is overly critical of the relative status of theory in finance. Because of its close relation to all parts of the enterprise, finance has been more self-conscious about its role and more concerned about identifying its potential contribution. An examination and review of other subject areas, including economic theory or any of its branches, such as public finance, or any of the other behavioral sciences, reveal the same kinds of uncertainties and disagreement on the identification of theories and principles.

Economics vs. Professional Content

The field of finance, like other business subjects, represents a segment of the behavioral sciences generally and the economic theory of the firm particularly. A subject focused on professional training emphasizes policies, procedures, and tools of analysis. A subject focused on behavioral sciences and economics emphasizes theories and im-

---

3 Paul M. Van Arsdell, "Discussion: Toward a Theory of Business Finance," *Journal of Finance,* X (May, 1955), 146.

4 Carl A. Dauten, "Toward a Theory of Business Finance: The Necessary Ingredients of a Theory of Business Finance," *The Journal of Finance,* X (May, 1955), 107.

plications for the operation of the society as a whole. Studies in finance have long emphasized the professional aspect of training and have had a very heavy institutional and descriptive content. Some finance people have felt that such emphasis has given inadequate attention to the economic theory of business finance. This has been well expressed by Professor Bosland:

> I would also make a plea for some new bridges between corporation finance and economic theory, particularly value and distribution theory. Here I would welcome a certain amount of duplication for the sake of emphasis, because the approaches are likely to be different, and anything that sharpens the analytical tools is to be encouraged. The general economic effects of methods of promotion, overcapitalization, fixed charges, dividend policies, reorganization and corporate expansion, for example, may receive too little emphasis both in courses in finance and in theory. Yet they may be more significant than some of the subject matter usually covered in both courses. The discussion of income distribution has its obvious ties to courses in labor as well.[5]

Professor Bosland suggests that economic theory helps make the study of business financial decisions more analytical. In addition, he feels that decisions in the area of business finance have important implications for the body of economic theories. With this point of view, I believe, all can agree. The question of the relative degree of emphasis, however, remains.

Principles vs. Institutions

For a long time the dominant writing in finance emphasized the description of financial institutions and institutions represented by finance instruments and their use. As our body of knowledge developed, the volume of descriptive material became more bulky until the chief textbook in finance, in its later editions, was published in two imposing volumes.[6] This led to increasing dissatisfaction well expressed in the following plaint:

> It is my impression that in many of our current courses and textbooks, we have become too complex, too encyclopedic, too demanding of memory at the expense of intellect. We may have overemphasized the role of the business giant, and in its complexities gone too far beyond the student's ability to comprehend the basic financial decisions necessary for such an organization.[7]

---

[5] Chelcie C. Bosland, "Materials and Methods of Teaching Business Finance (IV)," *Journal of Finance*, V (September, 1950), 287-88.

[6] Arthur S. Dewing, *The Financial Policy of Corporations* (New York: The Ronald Press Company, 1937 and 1943).

[7] Francis J. Calkins, "Materials and Methods of Teaching Business Finance (II)," *Journal of Finance*, V (September, 1950), 276.

Professor Calkins emphasizes that the test for inclusion of material in a finance textbook should be its relevance for financial decision making. But if an approach is taken which emphasizes the analytical ingredients for decision making, a vast body of descriptive material is unnecessary. This has been well expressed by Professor Hunt.

> For instance, although students must be taught the considerations involved in making a decision between debt and equity, there seems little need to add a multiplicity of detail concerning the almost infinite varieties of bonds and other types of security contracts. It is enough to introduce the student to a few of the major classifications and to tell him that the detail of a particular issue is subject to variations within the scope of the draftsman's imagination.[8]

There are important variables involved in formulating a financing contract. Elements of risk, income, control, and different options can be combined in varying degrees. Thus, it is impossible to encompass the full variety of finance contracts that could be formulated, and, furthermore, it is unnecessary to attempt to do so. If the fundamental elements of financial contracts are perceived, they can be combined in a large number of ways. But the issue of principles versus institutions is only one aspect of differing emphasis. Many disagreements arise from differences in the orientation or point of view from which the subject is approached. This point is considered in the following section.

Orientation of the Business Finance Subject Matter

Stockholders vs. Managers

For a long time, it was accepted without question that the business firm was operated from the standpoint of its owners. This point of view was applied in the analysis of the behavior of the large corporate enterprise. It was considered that the large corporate enterprise operated on behalf of the stockholders, even though ownership was diffused. Some economic writing argued that stockholders continued to be the real entrepreneurs in the business firm. This view is based on the reasoning that stockholders exercise the ultimate veto power. If they are dissatisfied with the operations of the business enterprise, they can sell their stock and invest in another corporate entity. Dissatisfaction with the operation of a corporation will subject it to the unfavorable verdict of the market place.[9] Other writers have em-

---

8 Pearson Hunt, "Materials and Methods of Teaching Business Finance (III)," *Journal of Finance*, V (September, 1950), 284.

9 Ben W. Lewis, "The Corporate Entrepreneur," *Quarterly Journal of Economics*, LI (May, 1937), 534-44.

phasized the separation of ownership and control.[10] The studies of R. A. Gordon established that the ownership position of managers is relatively small, probably less than 2 per cent. Yet, boards of directors are management dominated. In addition, the proxy machinery for the election of the board of directors is controlled by management. Thus, it is said that since ownership is separated from control, the orientation of the corporate enterprise is altered.

A wide series of consequences is said to follow. If control is separated from ownership, brilliant decisions that result in great successes provide no commensurate reward for management. On the other hand, bold decisions involve great risks, and failures come to the attention of superiors, stockholders, and the financial community. Since managers are not compensated in proportion to their successes, and since failures result in penalties, major risks are avoided. It has been said that this results in a "play-it-safe" policy by corporate managements, and, thus, that venturesome risk-taking is diminished in the American economy. It may be that the latter point of view fails to reflect actual compensation practices. High personal income tax rates following World War II and the Korean War stimulated the practice of giving top management stock options and other forms of profit participation. The considerable use of stock options and other profit-sharing arrangements thus provided them with a stake in the success of the enterprise. It may very well be, therefore, that, by the increased use of stock options in recent years, the entrepreneurial spirit has been again injected into corporate management.[11]

Other trends are said to have developed the requirement of a broader point of view. It is argued that the business firm represents an institution in the sociological sense. The institution has a role to play, involving a balancing of the various role-groups. The rising strength of the interests of the consumer, labor unions, and government represent forces against which stockholder interests must be balanced. This view has been appraised succinctly by Professor Donaldson.

> This concept of relative priority may be employed by professional management in relating the conflicting interests of stockholders, employees, customers, the general public, government, and so on to each

---

10 Robert A. Gordon, "Stockholdings of officers and directors in American industrial corporations," *Quarterly Journal of Economics*, L (August, 1936), 622-57; "Ownership by management and control groups in the large corporation," *Idem*, LII (May, 1938), 367-400; "Ownership and compensation as incentives to corporation executives," *Idem*, LIV (May, 1940), 455-73.

Also, A. A. Berle, Jr. and G. C. Means, *The Modern Corporation and Private Property* (New York: The Macmillan Company, 1944), pp. 119-25.

11 From this standpoint, the changes in the Revenues Act of 1964 which circumscribed the use of stock options has been unfavorable with regard to unifying interests of managers and owners.

other. Having abandoned the idea of *absolute* priority of the stockholder interest which existed only when management and ownership were one (and perhaps not even then), management continues to attach more weight to its responsibility to owners than to any other vested interest. This means, of course, that where a conflict of interest develops, management must determine how much of the stockholder interest will be sacrificed in order to behave "more responsibly" toward other interests such as the labor union or the customer. It does not mean, however, that either the direction of financial policy or the criterion by which achievement is measured has changed—only that the rate of progress in improving the rewards to the stockholder has been retarded in response to a greater awareness of other interests.[12]

Not only must the different points of view be represented, but, in addition, it is argued that the goals and criteria of decision making are fundamentally affected.[13] As a consequence of the difference in orientation, Professor Donaldson concludes that the stockholder point of view will be subordinate to that of management.

Thus the potential conflict between the professional manager and the professional stockholder is a latent problem, if not an active one, in every large-scale business. Every indication points to the emergence of the management (corporate entity) viewpoint as the dominant one in the long run. I mentioned at the outset that most academic writers have been on the side of the stockholder interest in discussions of how business ought to be run. My guess is that it will be financial theory and not management practice that will have to change if the two are to continue to have a valid relationship to each other.[14]

Views representing the opposite position have been expressed. One of the emerging themes in the practice of finance and in the increased responsibilities of financial managers is said to be stockholder relations.

Relationships between companies and their customers, employees, suppliers, and the general public have been undergoing revolutionary and sometimes planned development for many years—though usually long after the need has arisen. Sales has evolved into the broad, modern concept of the total marketing function. Good vendor relations are now recognized as good business. Employee and public relations have just about attained full membership in the family of primary business functions. Fifty years ago most employers gave employees a pay envelope every Saturday night and thought, "That's that." We know a lot more today, and we do a lot more for employees today, but until recently most companies treated share owners about the same way they treated employees some years ago.

---

12 Gordon Donaldson, "Financial Goals; Management vs. Stockholders," *Harvard Business Review*, May-June, 1963, p. 119.

13 *Ibid.*, p. 121.

14 *Ibid.*, p. 129.

Only in the past ten years has management concern for share-owner interests increased sharply. It is common knowledge that share-owners and outside-investor publics have not always received as much attention and policy consideration as have other groups. Although the investor of today may not be the completely forgotten man he once was, he is far from receiving sufficient public recognition for his contribution.[15]

This view holds that relationships with consumers, employees, suppliers, and the general public have long been recognized by business managers. Only recently has corporate management considered the need for communicating with shareholders. This responsibility is even broader in reflecting the needs of the company's particular shareholder groups.

Social vs. Managerial Viewpoint

In business schools, the professional viewpoint tends, typically, to be the dominant one in the study of business finance. The goal of the basic finance course varies somewhat, depending on whether the course is regarded as a terminal one or as a foundation for further study. In the latter case, there is also some uncertainty about whether the undergraduate course is preparation for further professional training or whether it is a foundation course for a research-oriented program. On the other hand, courses in business finance presented in an economics department may have a general economic or social point of view. Courses in the business schools may also take the same orientation. In a business school, the subject of business finance may also be studied from the standpoint of its impact on the operation of the economy. The behavior and performance of business firms are the keys to understanding the modern economic society. This view has been expressed exceptionally well by Professor Bosland, whose own writings have emphasized the social aspects of the operation of the corporate enterprise.

From the standpoint of public policy the most controversial issues are likely to be those centered around the large corporation. It is here that the engines of propaganda are at work and here the greatest misunderstanding is likely to develop. As I see it, the unique contribution that a course in corporation finance can make is the promotion of a better comprehension of the corporation in American life, as seen *both* from the inside out and the outside in. The financial problems of small business can best be introduced and appraised as they are projected against a broad background of the understanding of corporate financial policies in general. They constitute a part, but only a

---

15 L. E. Pettit, "Investor Relations: New Challenge to Management," *AMA Management Report No. 71* (New York: American Management Association, 1962), p. 67.

part, of the broader perspective, the greater emphasis upon ideas, and the increased attention to integration with allied courses in economics that I hope is gradually emerging in the teaching of college courses in corporation finance.[16]

This was also one of the central themes emphasized by Pearson Hunt in his challenging review of the 1942 edition of the Dewing book. Professor Hunt criticized the Dewing book for its rejection of the increased role of government instead of seeking to explain the proper limits and nature of the new government regulations:

> Another fundamental problem, with respect to which administrative policies are not so far advanced, includes both the questions of the bounds of appropriate financing and the question of control inherent in a system of widespread ownership. In this area such difficult issues are found as: the extent to which public agencies should limit the power of a corporation to issue bonds at will; or the freedom of a corporation to arrange for the concentration of its control into the hands of those who have invested relatively small amounts of funds, the problem that was first posed by Ripley and Brandeis.[17]

Professor Hunt emphasized the constraints represented by government rules and regulations which had increased with the coming of the New Deal legislation of the 1930's. In addition, he emphasized the social problems and issues that might be raised by the operation of the large corporate enterprise. He called attention particularly to the problem of the separation of ownership and control and the concentration of control in the hands of managers, not owners, of the corporate enterprise.

But the problems of corporate concentration, the separation of ownership and control, and the role of government regulations represent a relatively narrow scope of the finance subject compared to some of the more recent emphases.

> The emergence of national and international fiscal and trading and financial policies is of crucial importance to our corporations, causing them to become a major concern to financial officers.[18]

This point of view emphasizes that national fiscal and monetary policy have a great impact on financial decisions. Therefore, it is asserted that financial managers must concern themselves with national monetary and fiscal policy. In addition, international trading and financial policies increasingly have an impact on domestic policies. Therefore, the attention of the financial manager must be broadened

16 Chelcie C. Bosland, "Materials and Methods of Teaching Business Finance (IV)," *Journal of Finance*, V (September, 1950), 288.

17 Pearson Hunt, "The Financial Policy of Corporations," *Quarterly Journal of Economics*, LVII (February, 1943), 306-307.

18 Frank S. Capon, "Financial Management in the 70's," *Financial Executive*, October, 1963, p. 24.

to a world-wide scope. In fact, the other points emphasized by Mr. Capon include the whole complex of national and international economic and financial matters. The scope of the finance function and the finance subject matter is thus broadened to encompass the entire field of economics and management.

The Insider vs. the Outsider View

Another basis for criticism of the traditional business finance emphasis is that the entire subject of finance was treated from the point of view of the investment banker.[19] Attention was focused on the individual financing events which involved particularly the attention and services of the investment banker. This resulted in an organization of subject matter that was deficient in aspects that have been explained by Professor Solomon:

> . . . the sequence of treatment was built too closely around the episodic but infrequent phases during the life cycle of a hypothetical corporation during which external financial relations happen to be dominant. The argument in this connection is that over-emphasis on matters like promotion, incorporation, merger, consolidation, recapitalization, and reorganization left too little room for the problems of a normal growing company.[20]

Dissatisfaction with emphasis on the episodic and outsider point of view gave rise to a new stream of thinking in business finance represented by the Howard and Upton book.[21] The innovator here was Pearson Hunt who had called for such an approach in his 1943 article:

> Turning to the area of business practices, one can develop much new material of real significance by observing the problems of a firm as its treasurer would. All of us are too prone to remain on the outside looking in. Consider, for example, the limiting effects of a working capital shortage. . . . Or consider the problems of a treasurer who faces at the same time a demand for higher dividends and a union notice that an increased dividend will bring a strike for higher wages. Or consider the plight of the firm that stands ready to begin production on a war order as soon as a bank and surety company can agree upon what liens are to be taken, and how priorities shall be divided![22]

In this observation Pearson Hunt coined the phrase, "on the outside looking in," contrasting it to the point of view of the financial manager

---

[19] Ezra Solomon, *The Theory of Financial Management* (New York: Columbia University Press, 1963), p. 5.

[20] *Ibid.*, pp. 5-6.

[21] Bion B. Howard and Miller Upton, *Introduction to Business Finance* (New York: McGraw-Hill Book Company, 1953).

[22] Pearson Hunt, "The Financial Policy of Corporations," *Quarterly Journal of Economics*, LVII (February, 1943), 311.

concerned with the internal operations of the business firm. This view has often been equated with the working-capital approach, and the development of new studies in business finance tended to reflect it. They stated both explicitly and implicitly that working-capital management was a more significant aspect of the financial manager's responsibilities than were the episodes that occurred at widely separated, infrequent intervals. This controversy over the relative importance of the working-capital versus the episodic approach stimulated my survey of the activities of financial managers.[23] Commenting on the results of this survey, Professor Ketchum observed the following:

> Weston's article . . . indicates that financial executives, contrary to the newer school of thought on the subject, do not consider the things on which they spend the largest percentage of their time as being necessarily the most important things they do. They rank high in importance such activities as participation in long-range planning, revision and approval of terms of contracts for capital acquisitions, and the preparation of long-term budgets. These are duties which may take but a small portion of their working year.[24]

Thus, the survey found that most of the time of financial executives was spent on various aspects of working-capital management, reflecting their day-to-day responsibilities. However, the financial executives assigned greatest importance to the episodic decisions, such as long-term contracts for financing, mergers, and capital budgets. The individual financing episodes take on great importance, because, while such analysis may be made infrequently, they involve sums of considerable magnitude, and the consequences of the decisions have a continuing influence on the performance of the company over a long period of time.

A newer theme which is emerging in recent years is an approach which combines both views. In long-range planning, in the planning and control functions, and financial analysis of alternative product-market decisions, the finance function encompasses both the individual episodes and provides a framework for the day-to-day decisions involved in working-capital management. This focus was perceived clearly by Professor Halley in the early discussions of the scope of business finance:

> The question of internal administration vs. traditional material involves, first, a distinction between the two. The former can be regarded narrowly as concerned with day-to-day problems. Budgets, credits and collections, raising currently needed funds, relationships with banks, paying dividends and refunding a bond issue could well

---

23 J. Fred Weston, "Finance Function," *Journal of Finance,* IX, No. 3 (September, 1954), 265-82.

24 Marshall D. Ketchum, "Looking Around," *Harvard Business Review,* XXXIV, No. 1 (January-February, 1956), 132.

be examples of this concept. On the other hand, internal administration can also be considered as including much, if not all, of the material normally covered in traditional material, but looked at from the point of view of managerial decisions.[25]

Thus, working-capital management versus individual financial episodes may now be regarded as a false issue. Nor does a conflict exist between the view of the outsider looking in and that of the insider looking out. As the subsequent material will emphasize, modern business finance encompasses all of these points of view. In this connection, the approach which has thus far received relatively little attention is the financial history of an industry or the individual enterprise. Much could be gained by observing financial decisions in the broader framework of the evolution of the life cycle of both industries and individual firms.

Small Firm vs. Large Firm Financing

While business finance has been criticized for focusing on the problems of the large firm, there is no reason why this should be the emphasis of the subject matter. The principles of business finance are equally applicable to a large firm and a small firm. The tools of business finance, whether the working-capital approach, episodes, or the broader techniques of planning and control are emphasized, are equally needed by the large firm and the small. The environments in which these ideas will be applied will differ among large and small firms. The organization relationships involved in the large firm are, of course, more formal than those in the small firm. Many forms of communication and contact that are handled on a direct face-to-face or informal basis in the small firm must be formalized in the large firm. Much more paper work is involved in the operation of the large firm, and many more controls in the form of written reports are required in the effective conduct of the complex operations of the large enterprise. In principle, however, the same kinds of problems and decision areas must be handled by the small firm. Similarly, the distinction sometimes drawn between financing corporations and financing other forms of business enterprise serves no useful function. The boundaries between corporate and non-corporate forms of business enterprise are becoming increasingly blurred, especially under the impact of new tax regulations.

The instruments of finance can take a wide range of forms, and a wide range of forms will exist for both the non-corporate form of enterprise as well as the corporate. While the corporation has useful functions to perform and is the dominant form in which the business

[25] D. M. Halley, "Materials and Methods of Teaching Business Finance (I)," *Journal of Fnance*, V (September, 1950), 273.

enterprise is conducted in the United States when measured by dollars, non-corporate enterprise is also significant when measured by number of firms. The non-corporate enterprise is more numerous than the corporate. Numerically, corporations account for less than 15 per cent of the 4.6 million firms in the United States, but, measured by the fraction of national income generated, corporate business is by far the dominant form of enterprise, because it is characteristically the form employed by large scale enterprise. Hence, the proper subject of business finance encompasses both non-corporate business (because it is dominant in terms of numbers) and corporate enterprise (since it is a major form of enterprise in terms of dollar volume of business activity conducted).

Goals and Concepts of Financial Decision-Making

Thus far, the scope of the subject of business finance has been analyzed in terms of the different points of view from which the business finance field has been approached. We now turn to a further aspect of the fundamental issues in delineating the finance function. This represents the central goals and concepts of the subject.

Profit Maximization vs. Wealth Maximization

As a part of the general subject of economics, the goal of financial decision-making has generally been expressed in terms of what is maximized. However, economics employs some careless terminology. In the sections of economics books dealing with price theory, the goal of the firm is stated to be profit maximization. In other literature, particularly in capital theory, the goal is specified as maximizing wealth. Let us first consider, therefore, the nature of the profit maximization goal.

Four objections have been expressed to profit maximization as the goal of the business enterprise. The first objection is formal in nature. It relates to the problem of uncertainty. Since the future cannot be known well enough to express objective probability distributions of alternative possible returns, it is argued that it is not possible to maximize what cannot be known. In the face of true uncertainty, there is not an objective probability distribution that can be maximized. While this objection is valid and applies to expectations that cannot be expressed as probability distributions, the criticism would be equally valid against the wealth maximization goal.

The second objection is that most decisions involve a trade-off between expected return and risk. This is the essence of the portfolio problem. Characteristically, opportunities promising the possibility of higher expected yields are associated with greater risk. To recognize such a trade-off, wealth maximization is brought into the analysis. If greater expected returns are associated with higher risk, a higher capitalization rate would be applied to opportunities that involved greater risk. The combination of expected returns with risk variations and related capitalization rates can be fully expressed in the concept of wealth and utility maximization, but not in the concept of profit maximization.

The third objection is also related to the uncertainty factor. The decision-maker may have so little confidence in the estimates of future returns that may be achieved that he may forego attempting to maximize. Since whatever information or judgments he may have are subject to wide variations, he may prefer to "rest his case" when he has achieved some level that meets his needs, aspirations, or goals.[26]

In this connection, Professor Simon formulated the concept of "satisficing."

> In most psychological theories the motive to act stems from *drives,* and action terminates when the drive is satisfied. Moreover, the conditions for satisfying a drive are not necessarily fixed, but may be specified by an aspiration level that itself adjusts upward or downward on the basis of experience.
>
> If we seek to explain business behavior in the terms of this theory, we must expect the firm's goals to be not maximizing profit, but attaining a certain level or rate of profit, holding a certain share of the market or a certain level of sales. Firms would try to "satisfice" rather than to maximize.[27]

Space does not permit full treatment of the maximizing versus the "satisficing" argument. The satisficing goal is appropriate for a behavioral theory of the firm and is perfectly manageable. It is not necessary to make mutually exclusive choices between wealth maximization and wealth satisficing. Satisficing is primarily a short-run search strategy and relates to the cost of search. If information and search costs are low, additional effort will be made to maximize. Where information and search costs are high, additional effort to seek to maximize promises little additional net gains, so the decision maker may be said to satisfice. Thus when information and search costs are taken into account, the differences between satisficing and maximizing may be small or nonexistent.

The fourth objection to profit or wealth maximization is that it is too narrowly centered. The complaint is that such a maximization criterion fails to take into consideration the roles and interests of government, labor unions, and other participants in the enterprise process. Much has been written on whether the maximization criterion

---

[26] Herbert A. Simon, "Theories of Decision-Making in Economics and Behavioral Science," *American Economic Review,* XLIX (June, 1959), 253-83.

[27] *Ibid.,* p. 262-63.

from the standpoint of the shareholders of a firm is any longer appropriate in a world of cooperating agents, each with a limited role.

Professor Solomon has handled this issue in a well-reasoned manner. He argues that it is useful to distinguish between profits and profitability.[28] Maximization of profit in the sense of maximizing the wealth "accrual" to stockholders is clearly an unreal motive. How the wealth of the firm is shared among the participants can be subject to considerable argument. On the other hand, profitability maximization in the sense of using resources to yield economic values higher than the joint values of the inputs required is a useful goal.[29] The distribution of the profitability achieved by outputs greater than input values involves another set of considerations. Thus, a proper goal of financial management is wealth maximization.

But what of the other interest groups or other possible goals of management? Professor Solomon handles this issue in the following terms:

> But what if management has other motives, such as maximizing sales or size, growth or market share, or their own survival, or peace of mind? These operating goals do not necessarily conflict with the operating goal of wealth-maximization. Indeed, a good case could be made for the thesis that wealth-maximization also maximizes the achievement of these other objectives. But the point of issue is what if there is a conflict? What, for example, if management's quest for its own peace of mind or for some other goal consistently leads it to reject operating decisions that should be accepted by the wealth-maximizing criterion? [30]

The answer Professor Solomon gives is that legally management represents the owners. If they do not perform effectively or satisfactorily, managements will be replaced sooner or later. He concludes, therefore, that maximization of wealth provides a useful and meaningful objective as the basic guideline by which financial decisions will be evaluated.

The broader viewpoint takes into account the relations between different investment opportunities. This brings us to portfolio analysis. Portfolio analysis presents combinations of higher risk and higher expected returns with lower risk and lower expected returns. The final decision depends on the preferences of the decision maker. Thus utility maximization is the broadest of the maximization criteria. Thus profit maximization and wealth maximization can be joined by subsuming them under utility maximization. The timeless world of profit maximization can then be compared with the allocation of

---

[28] Solomon, *op. cit.*, p. 17.
[29] *Ibid.*, p. 18.
[30] *Ibid.*, p. 24.

resources over time involved in wealth maximization. The allocation of resources over time is a problem that is central to finance.

Cash Flow vs. Wealth Maximization

In contrast to maximizing or satisficing objectives, still a fifth view of the function of business finance is to analyze cash flows. This is the fund flow or cash flow approach to business finance. In one form or another, this has been the central emphasis of books in business finance. This approach can be illustrated by reference both to a standard book which in its early editions represented the traditional emphasis of finance and a later approach.

> Business finance can be broadly defined as the activity concerned with the planning, raising, controlling, and administering of funds used in the business.[31]

The second point of view is, however, expressed in a book which was developed to represent the working capital emphasis.

> In its simplest sense finance refers to those activities involved in seeing that an individual or organization has the cash with which to pay its bills promptly.[32]

This point of view was also emphasized early by Hunt, when he stated:

> In analyzing the decisions of entrepreneurs, economists seem prone to forget that the financial condition of a firm not only affects its ability to pay its debts, but extends its influence to other decisions as well. Anyone who has examined the effects of the great need for working capital which has been created by war production orders can never again omit consideration of liquidity, as it affects willingness to expand, availability of funds to replace high cost equipment that can still be operated, and willingness to enter agreements with labor leading to the elimination of lay-offs. Examples might be multiplied, but the conclusion is clear. The spending of a business is influenced by its working capital position in ways that are subject to useful generalization. Here is an opportunity to weave corporate history with the economics of variable costs, to the advantage of all. One point seems worthy of special emphasis, since it is so often missed by general theorists. The occurrence of bankruptcy frequently frees funds for spending on capital assets or on wages, since it relieves the struggling company of the necessity of meeting debt payments at least for a time.[33]

---

[31] H. Guthmann and H. Dougall, *Corporate Financial Policy* (Englewood Cliffs, N.J.: Prentice-Hall, Inc., 1940), p. 1.

[32] M. Upton and B. Howard, *op. cit.*, p. 3.

[33] Pearson Hunt, *op. cit.*, p. 310.

While the flow of cash or funds is a central concern of financial management, it cannot be pursued independently. One point of view in this connection has been expressed effectively by Professor Van Arsdell:

> In suggesting *capital* rather than *cash* as the "heart of the finance function" I am not intentionally or seriously quarrelsome with Professor Dauten or others of our associates in this field—including Professors Howard and Upton—who emphasize the cash flow approach. I feel that the capital, or capital flow, approach is appropriately broader not only in terms of financial management but in terms of the fundamental objective of the business firm as a productive, economic unit. As one example only, the capital impairment problem is certainly one of business finance; its solution transcends, from this standpoint, the scope of the cash accounts.[34]

To summarize and conclude, the analysis of the flow of cash is not as much an objective as a *constraint* on the maximizing goals which may be formulated by the firm. The analysis of the flow of cash emphasizes the liquidity requirements of the business enterprise. Liquidity represents a device for dealing with risk or uncertainty. Hence, through liquidity analysis, a firm may seek to minimize particular elements of risk or uncertainty. However, it represents at best a negative constraint rather than a positive goal of business activity.

Specific Finance Functions vs. Generic Management Responsibilities

Whatever involves cash or funds is sometimes said to represent the proper domain of financial decisions. This had been well expressed by Mr. Alvin Brown:

> All decisions are financial, either because they directly affect the expenditure of money, or because they indirectly affect expenditures by consuming or disposing of effort, facilities, or material, all of which cost money. A decision to improve toilet and locker facilities may begin from a proper concern for the health and comfort of employees, but it requires an expenditure, and every expenditure affects the earnings of the enterprise. All decisions are financial because you cannot conceive of one that does not affect, in one way or another, and in some degree, the earnings of the enterprise.[35]

The definition of finance as anything that involves the dollar sign is too broad, however.[36] It expresses an element of truth in so far as it recognizes that financial management is concerned not only with

---

[34] Paul M. Van Arsdell, "Discussion: Toward a Theory of Business Finance," *Journal of Finance*, X (May, 1955), 145.

[35] Alvin Brown, *Financial Approach to Industrial Operations* (New York: Society for the Advancement of Management, 1957), p. 7.

[36] Solomon, *op. cit.*, p. 2.

specific financial management functions but with the over-all management of the business enterprise. Finance is involved with both the compilation and analysis of accounting data. Financing is also included in the evaluation of many decisions of the business enterprise. At some point, all the record keeping and financial information must be coordinated into over-all budgets, plans, and policies for the business enterprise. Financial managers are likely to be involved in these decisions. Such a complete involvement of financial managers in the operations of the enterprise is, however, distinct from saying that any decision that involves dollars is a responsibility of financial management.

A related position is that recent developments in economics and business have placed the financial manager in a central position in the business firm. This has been well expressed in an article in which the role of the financial officer is said to have been enhanced by a "management revolution":

> There is a tide in the affairs of the financial executive. What must he do to take it at the turn?
>
> First, recognize this management revolution in all its implications.
>
> Second, realize that the developments of financial management over the past two decades have prepared him, better than any other officer, to provide the president with the planning and control tools he needs.[37]

Since most business activities involve the use of funds, financial management must have cognizant involvement in all of the other activities which take place. Both awareness and coordination of other activities is required. This view has been stated by Professor Donaldson:

> Because most business activities involve the utilization and/or the generation of funds, important management decisions in all areas inevitably have financial implications. Not only must these implications be understood and taken into account in reaching a balanced decision, but varying interests must be coordinated if the company is to achieve financial success.[38]

Another aspect of the interrelationship between finance and other areas is the need for coordinating planning in the basic business activities of the firm and their interrelationship with cash planning. As Professor Williams has observed,

> . . . effective cash planning must come after, not before, effective general planning for the company, since all phases of operation

---

[37] T. F. Bradshaw, "The Place and Status of the Financial Executive Today," *The Financial Executive's Job*, Financial Management Series No. 99 (New York: American Management Association, 1952), p. 22.

[38] Gordon Donaldson, "Looking Around; Finance for the Nonfinancial," *Harvard Business Review*, XXXVIII (January-February, 1960), 33.

affect the cash position. Is not the treasurer who needs to do careful cash planning but cannot get his associates in manufacturing, procurement, etc., to commit themselves to plans in a poor position to do effective cash planning? [39]

In his discussion, Professor Williams went on to recognize that the operations of companies are subject to uncertainty and fundamental changes. He showed further that the need for cash planning is greatest in companies subject to the largest amount of unanticipated change. Budgets and plans are required in order to provide a point of reference when changes cause adjustments.[40]

This idea has also been expressed by Professor Solomon. His statement provides an interim summary of a consensus on the nature of the finance function.

> . . . Financial management is properly viewed as an integral part of over-all management rather than as a staff specialty concerned with fund-raising operations. In this broader view the central issue of financial policy is the wise use of funds, and the central process involved is a rational matching of the advantages of potential uses against the cost of alternative potential sources so as to achieve the broad financial goals which an enterprise sets for itself. The underlying fund-using proposals which originate within the operating departments of an enterprise are still assumed as given. So are present and prospective conditions in technology and in the markets for goods, services, and capital. Given these data, the function of financial management is to review and control decisions to commit or recommit funds to new or ongoing uses. Thus, in addition to raising funds, financial management is directly concerned with production, marketing, and other functions within an enterprise whenever decisions are made about the acquisition or destruction of assets.[41]

This conception of finance emphasizes that marketing, production, new product decisions, etc., all involve not only the flow of cash but also an evaluation of alternative resource allocation possibilities. Finance must consider a broad range of business decisions for their cash flow implications. But, in addition, as specialists in evaluation of alternative uses of funds, financial managers are involved in evaluation of resource allocation choices. Finance is, therefore, concerned with the following wide range of areas.

1. Size of the firm
2. Rate of growth
3. Asset mix

[39] Charles M. Williams, "Discussion: Toward a Theory of Business Finance," *Journal of Finance*, X (May, 1955), 150.
[40] *Ibid.*, p. 150.
[41] Solomon, *op. cit.*, pp. 2-3.

4. Product mix
5. Product evaluation, financial analysis, and review of alternative product-market areas
6. Financing mix
7. Fixed versus variable cost mix
8. Make-or-buy alternatives

Analysis of these decision areas involves (1) information flow, (2) analysis of information, (3) feedback and monitoring, (4) an adjustment mechanism and (5) implementation of changes. All of this is within the framework of wealth maximization for the enterprise. The following chapters develop the significance of this orientation of finance.

The Evolution of the
Finance Function

THE PREVIOUS chapter which discussed the basic issues in delineating the scope of the finance function and the finance field has left many important matters unresolved. The following chapters will attempt to reduce disagreements on the major issues. The present chapter seeks to provide a foundation by placing the finance function in an historical perspective.

Fundamental Propositions

The evolution of the finance function's relationship to historical developments can best be understood if three general propositions are accepted. These generalizations may be regarded as the philosophical and methodological assumptions of this book. They are:

(1) The history of economic thought reflects the pressing problems of the day. In 1776, Adam Smith wrote how the wealth of the British nation might be increased by departing from the prevailing mercantilist doctrines. John Maynard Keynes' *The General Theory of Employment, Interest and Money* (1936) sought to find a solution for the severe world-wide depression of the 1930's. In the subject matter of finance, responses to the urgent problems of the day may also be seen.

(2) The second proposition is that necessity is a less important factor in inducing invention than is the mounting inventory of knowl-

edge which makes it possible to achieve proximate developments. Necessity is omnipresent and pervasive. Achievement, however, is based on the knowledge, tools, and concepts required to solve pressing problems. In finance, new advances have been linked to the development of theories and tools in related fields.

(3) The third proposition concerns the development of theory and its application to finance. It states that whatever is convenient and appropriate to the *ceteris paribus* (other things being equal) box is a matter of the nature of the problem and of the variables undergoing the greatest change and having the greatest impact on final results. In finance, the changing economic and managerial environment has made it possible to give relatively little attention to some aspects of the subject matter at some times and to focus attention on these items at others.

These propositions have relevance for the understanding of the evolution of the finance function and may be made more meaningful by some explicit documentation presented initially in outline form (*see* Table 2-1). This tabulation includes three major columns: the time period, the major economic and industrial developments which occurred, and the impact of these developments on the content of the finance field.

The Turn of the Century

A systematic study of financial management began at the turn of the century. This was associated with the major consolidation movement in the United States associated with the emergence of national markets after the completion of cross-continental railroad networks in the late 1880's. By the end of the merger movement in the early 1900's, 305 industrial combinations had been put together. In 78 of these industrial complexes, the resulting firm controlled half or more of the total output in the industry.[1] Financing these large industrial aggregates brought management face to face with important problems of capital structure. The components of the large trusts were relatively few in number. The average number of plants or firms brought together by the 305 large trusts was 16. Over half of the consolidations, 183, were formed from eight or fewer plants or firms, and about one-third were formed from four or fewer plants or firms.[2] The resulting firms were large in relation to the size of the economy and industries.

Of great importance was the selection of capital structure and the major financing episodes which followed. Professor Arthur Stone

---

[1] J. F. Weston, *The Role of Mergers in the Growth of Large Firms* (Berkeley: University of California Press, 1953), pp. 31-32.

[2] *Ibid.*, pp. 32-33.

Table 2-1: Outline of the Evolution of the Finance Function

A. Time Period	B. Economic and Industrial Developments	C. Impact on Content of Finance Field
Turn of the Century	1. Consolidation movement	1. Capital structure 2. Major financing episodes
1920's	1. Burst of new industries 2. Mergers to round out marketing lines 3. High profit margins	1. Financial structure 2. Some planning and control 3. Liquidity considerations
1930's	1. Severe economic recession 2. Wave of reorganization and bankruptcy 3. New Deal Legislation of 1930's	1. Errors of unsound financial structure 2. Solvency and liquidity 3. Financial rehabilitation 4. Social controls
Early 1950's	1. Rapid expansion 2. Reestablishment of monetary policy 3. Apprehension of postwar recession	1. Emphasis on cash flows vs. profitability 2. De-emphasis of financial ratio analysis 3. Use of internal financial management procedures: aging receivables, cash budget forecasts
Late 1950's Early 1960's	1. Improved profit opportunities 2. Increased pace of technological change 3. New industries 4. Stock market premium on growth 5. Large scale computers 6. Increased importance of international trade and balance of payments considerations	1. Capital budgeting analysis of opportunities 2. Cost of capital analysis to determine investment hurdles 3. Planning and control to increase profit growth regardless of sales growth 4. Mass data processing and simulation techniques 5. Emphasis on major financial institutions and price level movements 6. International business and finance

Dewing wrote an early classic on finance in 1914.[3] He studied the promotions and failures which resulted in reorganizations in the early 1900's. His analysis of the fundamental causes of failure emphasized unsound financial management as a major contributing factor.

---

[3] Arthur Stone Dewing, *Corporate Promotions and Reorganizations* (Cambridge, Mass.: Harvard University Press, 1930).

They failed because their earnings were inadequate for the load put upon them. If the load was especially burdensome by reason of heavy fixed charges and unwarranted dividend payments, the failure was all the more certain. The direct cause of failure in every instance was the deflection of working capital to the payment of interest and dividends. Beneath this, as the fundamental cause, was the lack of judgment of promoters in placing bonds upon an untried industrial enterprise and the lack of conservatism of the early management in paying dividends without due regard to sound principles of finance. Every corporation discussed in this volume paid out interest or dividends in the face of falling earnings, and none need have suffered serious financial difficulties had the amounts paid in interest and dividends been conserved.[4]

Of great significance was the selection of the form of capital structure. Dewing notes that companies with smaller debt burdens were in a stronger position.

It is largely because of these clearly recognized fluctuations of trade, that a sound financial policy dictates the use of stock rather than bonds. And it should be remarked at this point that the strength of our so-called "industrial trusts" lies partly in the fact that the majority of them were promoted without bonds. But when foolish promoters had once over-loaded a corporation with liabilities bearing fixed charges, it became the duty of the subsequent management to get along as best it could. A default in bond interest payments was very disastrous to the credit of a corporation, as well as to the market price of its securities. It was disastrous to its trade as well.[5]

This intensive analysis of the early history of large corporations greatly impressed Professor Dewing. The choice of capital structure was seen to be of great significance. Dividend policy also had an impact on the liquidity and subsequent strength of the corporation. The central concern of financial management in the environment of the sharp economic crisis at the turn of the century was to *preserve* the firm against bankruptcy and reorganization. Dewing's subsequent textbooks in corporate finance set the pattern for what is now referred to as the traditional corporate finance approach. Because the early consolidations involved large aggregates, the nature and terms of the financial contracts were matters of critical significance. This resulted in the heavy institutional and descriptive emphasis of traditional business finance.

The 1920's

In the 1920's, a burst of new industries came upon the economic scene. In the explosive rise, some of the most significant of these were

---

4 *Ibid.*, pp. 557-8.
5 *Ibid.*, p. 553.

the radio, chemical, automobile, and steel industries. Large-scale national advertising emerged, and distribution methods were improved. Mergers were employed to round out marketing lines. Profit margins were high, but the inventory recession and sharp price declines of 1920-1921 again emphasized the importance of financial structure in financial studies. Tight money and inventory price fluctuations stimulated increased attention to liquidity considerations.

Profit margins were favorable and improved during the years 1923-1929. The book by McKinsey and Meech combined accounting and financial elements in developing the theory and practice of budgeting and is surprisingly modern in many of its sections.[6] It emphasized control of the day-to-day operations of the firm as an on-going enterprise. The McKinsey and Meech book might have initiated a new trend in business finance thinking, but the events of the 1930's renewed the overwhelming emphasis on liquidity and a sound capital structure in formulating financial policy.

The 1930's

The recession which began in 1929 was unprecedented in its duration and severity. In the business field, it carried in its train a great wave of financial reorganizations and bankruptcies. A scramble for liquidity took place. The public began to claim their deposits from the commercial banks. The banks in turn reduced their lines of credit outstanding; loans were not renewed and in some cases were called. Forced inventory liquidations ensued. Prices declined and the inventory liquidations did not provide sufficient funds to meet obligations. The importance of liquidity was demonstrated for the second time during the decade.

With the reduced rate of business activity, losses resulted. Fixed financial charges were especially burdensome. The adverse consequences of trading-on-the-equity were illustrated. In the public utility holding company systems, financial leverage had been magnified through the pyramiding of layers of intermediate entities. When operating revenue declined, the systems could not support the heavy burdens of financial charges, and a devastating collapse of the far-flung systems followed. In the railroad industry, most railroads were able to cover current operating expenses, but debilitating deficits resulted from the overhang of heavy, fixed financial charges resulting from high debt ratios. As a consequence, virtually the entire railroad industry went through reorganization.

These events of the 1930's seemed to underline the importance of traditional business finance. The errors of unsound financial structure,

---

6 J. O. McKinsey and Stuart P. Meech, *Controlling the Finances of a Business* (New York: The Ronald Press Company, 1923).

particularly the consequences of heavy debt charges, were again drama-
tized. The importance of the emphasis that traditional business finance
placed on individual financial episodes and the analysis of financial
structure was reaffirmed.

Planning and control under such circumstances were of relatively
minor importance. It was understood that the firm would do as well as
it could do to choose its market and to expand its operations. But
in the depressed economy it was difficult to find any attractive market,
and if sales fell by as much as 50 per cent (the decline in Gross National
Product between 1929 and 1932), operating efficiency was then less
important than minimizing fixed charges of all kinds. In the face of
such a decline in revenues, solvency and liquidity became important
commandments of the financial manager.

The wave of reorganizations and bankruptcies produced a number
of publications and case studies. Financial rehabilitation became an
important part of finance. Firms had either experienced a financial
crisis or lived in fear of it. Traditional business finance was, therefore,
underscored with increased attention to reorganization and bankruptcy. These events established the importance of sound financial
structure as a preventive for financial embarrassment.

The turn of the century, 1920-21, and 1929-33—three deep, searing,
and traumatic experiences with debt—go a long way toward explaining the continuing "irrational aversion to debt on the part of corporate managements." It appears that business firms incur long-term
debt only when absolutely necessary to finance rapid expansion. They
seek to retire debt as soon as possible. Many writers have asserted
that the maximizing principles of normative business finance have little
realism or relevance. They argue that financial managers simply seek
to "play it safe." In the light of the devastating experience of the
early 1930's still within the memory of mature business executives,
such a policy toward debt may simply represent an illustration of the
"minimax principle"—minimize the maximum risk exposure. In view
of the difficulty of postulating the degree of severity and general economic fluctuations, a policy which protects the firm against a disaster
similar to that experienced in recent decades represents highly rational behavior in a highly uncertain world.

Another major theme was introduced during this decade. The dramatic failure of the economic and business system naturally led to a
search for the villains. Large-scale business enterprise was one group
singled out. In a profitable, growing, and optimistic environment, low
liquidity and high leverage are labeled financial daring. In a period
of economic disaster, they are labeled financial chicanery. The deli-
cate and intricate financial relationships are based on confidence and
on favorable momentum for their success. The economic catastrophe
of the 1930's was regarded as evidence of the inability of private business to function effectively in the absence of a more active role by

the government. The New Deal legislation of the 1930's changed the legal and institutional framework in which business operated. The New Deal legislation included the securities acts, the banking acts, and the public utility holding company laws. All of these were particularly significant for business finance.

Therefore, another important factor and one to which Pearson Hunt called attention in the early 1940's was the burgeoning framework of government laws, regulations, and controls.[7] In some respects, it is curious that aside from some excellent individual treatments of this aspect of business finance, it never seems to have become a significant segment of finance textbook literature.[8] Two reasons may account for this. The private financial manager is not the one who determines these regulations, and the nature and impact of the regulations is best understood in connection with specific financial instruments or arrangements. Therefore, the framework of social regulation is covered in connection with the traditional topics rather than as a separate subject. To the extent that federal social control themes could be identified, such as the separation of ownership and control or the arguments *pro* and *con* federal incorporation laws, finance books treat them in separate chapters.

The 1940's

The 1940's were, of course, dominated by World War II and its immediate aftermath. All activity was subordinated and directed to the tremendous war effort. The magnitude of the involvement made private and individual decisions of secondary consideration. A large number of industries shifted to production for the defense effort. The conduct of the war required specialized products without peacetime uses. The specialized investments required to produce these goods required large sums of money. The use of these facilities was of uncertain duration, with little or no application for the peacetime economy. It was, therefore, necessary to finance such programs primarily by government resources. Financial officers of firms were involved in arranging the financing programs with government help.

Also important was negotiation of the terms of the government contracts and the various types of repricing provisions in these contracts. Formal contract renegotiation reviews were conducted on an annual basis. Special problems of contract termination claims began during the war as requirements changed according to the major areas of combat which shifted successively from North Africa to Italy to France

---

[7] Pearson Hunt, "The Financial Policy of Corporations," *Quarterly Journal of Economics,* LVII (February, 1943).

[8] For an excellent development of this theme see Chelcie C. Bosland, *Corporate Finance and Regulation* (New York: The Ronald Press Company, 1949).

and to the Pacific. Each theatre required different equipment and weapons. The large volume of operations in wartime programs required attention to short-term working capital management.

As the flow of funds from sales to the Department of Defense began to cover working-capital requirements, the liquidation of commercial inventories and investments provided increased funds. Mindful of the post-war recessions of 1920-21 and of 1929-32, many firms reduced their long-term debts since these were related to their civilian business which for many firms had been either curtailed or stopped. For business firms as a whole, liquidity increased during the war period. Nevertheless, considerable apprehension existed over the ability to finance the conversion to peacetime production. The problem of financing the reconversion in industries, such as consumer durable goods, was of major proportions. In industries such as these, the production of goods had been stopped during the war, and large post-war demands were anticipated to satisfy the postponed needs of the population.

In the period immediately after World War II, financing the expansion of capacity and the working-capital growth associated with the growth of sales of peacetime products assumed crucial proportions for private financial policy. The great emphasis was on obtaining large increments of capital financing. The Employment Act of 1946 promised increased attention to economic stability in the economy. Yet, experience provided no assurance that these new policies and the built-in stabilizers (unemployment insurance, social security payments, personal and corporate tax yields with anti-cyclical variations) would in fact bring greater stability to the American economy. So corporate finance continued to be concerned with the necessity for selecting financial structures that would be able to withstand the stresses of the post-war adjustments.

Early 1950's

The early 1950's were years of rapid economic expansion continuously clouded with the threat of a major post-war recession. Throughout the vigorous growth of the early post-World War II period, influential opinion emphasized the dangers of the primary and secondary post-war recessions, paralleling the inventory recession of 1920-21 and the major collapse of 1929-33.

The vigorous expansion was confronted with the reestablishment of monetary policy after the famous Accord of March, 1951. Rising labor costs led to the substitution of capital equipment for labor. The rapid growth of firms coupled with a depressed equity market in the early 1950's and a tightening money market placed great emphasis on the conservation of cash. Cash flows came to take a coordinate emphasis with profitability. The preoccupation of financial management with the "outsider looking in" and hence financial ratio analysis, the tool of the outside analyst, was deemphasized. The uses and application of internal financial management procedures received increased attention. The role of cash budget forecasting received vigorous development. Internal managerial controls, such as aging receivables, analysis of purchases, and the application of inventory controls, were emphasized. The nature of the finance field began to undergo significant changes.

Late 1950's and Early 1960's

By the late 1950's, profit opportunities in mature industries began to narrow. The increased pace of research and development opened new industries and industrial segments. In these new segments, firms were created and experienced explosive growth. The dramatic achievements of the new science firms resulted in a rapid increase in the market prices of their stock. These price increases were more rapid than the market as a whole. The limited profit opportunities in traditional industrial activity stimulated the theory of capital budgeting. With relatively tight money and a limited range of opportunities, careful assessment of resource allocation became of increased importance. The narrowing of the margin between prospective profitability and the cost of funds stimulated cost of capital analysis to determine appropriate investment hurdles. The dramatic premiums placed on profit growth stimulated techniques of planning and control to increase profit growth regardless of sales growth.

Of great importance in the area of technological change is the development of the large-scale computer which facilitated increased data processing on a level never before contemplated. Thus, important aspects of inventory and receivables control can now be achieved. Increased scope for the effectiveness of profitability and of planning and control has now been realized. The recognition of the interconnection between all parts of the business enterprise can now be encompassed by the information processing capabilities of the computer. In addition, the entire enterprise operations can be simulated. As a consequence, interrelationships between subjects are becoming closer. The systems approach to business management breaks down traditional labels of specific management functions, such as production, marketing and finance.

Another major factor in the economic environment has been the increased importance of balance of payments in formulating the nation's economic policies. In international competition, effective control of costs and successful creation of attractive products have become of increased importance. The scope of business enterprise is broadened to the international environment. There has been increased recognition that the large scale American market made possible economies of mass production. International markets will make possible further advances in economies of large-scale operations. In the international environment, financial institutions and instruments take on a wide variety of forms. A broadened analytical framework is required to understand and to encompass the wide range of characteristics of the emerging international economy. Differential price level movements in different countries make it impossible to assume relative stability in price levels. Policies for dealing with differential changes in prices and costs must be formulated.

The finance field thus enters into an era of dramatic and revolutionary change. It is a period in which profit margins and opportunities are narrowing in some areas as they are developing in others. The technology of modern management makes possible a revolution in tools and concepts. The improvement in information technology is causing the traditional compartments of managerial functions to become blurred. In this period of rapid change, it becomes particularly important to reassess the appropriate scope and role of the finance function to provide a solid foundation for understanding its nature and relations to other fields of study. To achieve these objectives, some basic methodological issues are next considered.

```
333333333333333333333333333333333333333333333333333333333333333333333333333333333333
333333333333333333333333333333333333333333333333333333333333333333333333333333333333
3333333333333333333333333333333333333   333   333   333333333333333333333333333333333
3333333333333333333333333333333333333   333   333   333333333333333333333333333333333
3333333333333333333333333333333333333   333   333   333333333333333333333333333333333
3333333333333333333333333333333333333   333   333   333333333333333333333333333333333
3333333333333333333333333333333333333   333   333   333333333333333333333333333333333
3333333333333333333333333333333333333   333   333   333333333333333333333333333333333
3333333333333333333333333333333333333   333   333   333333333333333333333333333333333
3333333333333333333333333333333333333   333   333   333333333333333333333333333333333
3333333333333333333333333333333333333   333   333   333333333333333333333333333333333
333333333333333333333333333333333333333333333333333333333333333333333333333333333333
333333333333333333333333333333333333333333333333333333333333333333333333333333333333
```

The Methodology of the
Finance Field

ANY DISCUSSION of methodology must begin with the elder Keynes who made a persuasive case for the importance of methodology.

> . . . a certain impatience is sometimes felt when any such discussion is proposed. What we want, it is said, is not any more talk about method, but rather useful applications of the right method; let us increase our actual stock of economic truths, instead of indulging in barren disputes about the way in which economic truths are to be attained. To this objection the logician might reply that the enquiry has at any rate a logical, even if it has not an economic, significance. But it has also an economic significance. A moment's consideration will show that, from the point of view of political economy itself, it is of material importance that its scope and method should be rightly understood.[1]

The greatest value of the scope and method of the field is its contribution to the development of a theory with which to approach the "facts" of the subject matter. As Keynes expressed it,

> Even when we are engaged in the mere collection and registration of events, it is often advantageous, as Jevons has pointed out in the case of the physical observer, that our attention should be guided by theoretical anticipations. Industrial phenomena are exceedingly complex,

---

[1] John Neville Keynes, *The Scope and Method of Political Economy* (London: Macmillan & Co., Ltd., 1890, reprinted 1930), p. 285.

and unless we know what special facts to look for, it is quite possible that some of the most vital circumstances may fail to attract our notice. Knowledge of cause and effect in the economic world is, accordingly, of assistance for discriminating between the facts to be specially noted and those that may without risk of error be disregarded.[2]

The other early great treatise on methodology in economics was formulated by Professor Lionel Robbins who summarized the nature of economic analysis in the following manner.

In the light of all that has been said the nature of economic analysis should now be plain. It consists of deductions from a series of postulates, the chief of which are almost universal facts of experience present whenever human activity has an economic aspect, the rest being assumptions of a more limited nature based upon the general features of particular situations or types of situations which the theory is to be used to explain.[3]

By their classic studies, Keynes and Robbins have had important influence on the method of economics. The resulting approach to economic problems can be summarized briefly.

The Economic Theory of the Firm

In the economic theory of the firm, the goal-objective has been described as maximizing net revenue, given product and factor prices and a technologically determined production function. The existing economic theory of the firm focuses on analyzing the conditions for maximizing net revenue and analyzing causes of shifts in equilibrium positions. At equilibrium, the marginal rates of substitution between products or factors are equal to the ratios of their prices. In general, demand curves are negatively sloped and supply curves are positively sloped. The concepts of oligopoly and monopolistic competition modify some assumptions about the characteristics of demand and supply functions but do not change the basic decision processes.

The traditional objection to economic theory questions the basic assumptions of the psychology of economic man. The individual is presented as a rational "pain-and-pleasure calculating machine." Most of the charges that economic theory is based on an unsound theory of the psychology of the individual, however, are exaggerated or misdirected. A clear defense of the limited psychological assumptions of economics was clearly stated by Lionel Robbins over thirty years ago.

The general absurdity of the belief that the world contemplated by the economist is peopled only by egotists or "pleasure machines" should

---

[2] *Ibid.*, p. 3.

[3] Lionel Robbins, *An Essay on the Nature & Significance of Economic Science* (London: Macmillan & Co., Ltd., 1932, reprinted 1952), p. 100.

be sufficiently clear from what has been said already. The fundamental concept of economic analysis is the idea of relative valuations; and, as we have seen, while we assume that different goods have different values at different margins, we do not regard it as part of our problem to explain why these particular valuations exist. We take them as data. So far as we are concerned, our economic subjects can be pure egoists, pure altruists, pure ascetics, pure sensualists or—what is much more likely—mixed bundles of all these impulses. The scales of relative calculation are merely a convenient formal way of exhibiting certain permanent characteristics of man as he actually is. Failure to recognise the primacy of these valuations is simply a failure to understand the significance of the last sixty years of Economic Science.[4]

As Professor Robbins suggests, economics does not take a position on the relative role of money incentives *vs.* other psychological influences. Economics implies only that in consumption and production decisions monetary incentives perform some role. Economics suggests that if a market position is in equilibrium, a variation of the monetary incentive is likely to alter the equilibrium valuation.[5] Furthermore, economics does not assert that the monetary incentive is the most important influence in such situations. In different economies under varied circumstances, economics acknowledges that a wide variety of cultural influences and cultural variations may dominate human behavior. In the production and consumption decisions of a society or culture, economic factors will exert some influence.

The broader concept of utility maximization is helpful here. Utility maximization is a concept which may encompass economic, psychological, and other influences. Profit maximization or wealth maximization may then be viewed as special cases in which, for simplicity, utility is treated as a single valued function of profit or wealth.

Behavioral Theory of the Firm

In recent years, a rival to the economic theory of the firm has been developed—namely, the behavioral theory of the firm.[6] The behavioral theory of the firm asserts that economics does not deal with the organization and control problems which influence the decision process in the firm. Summarized briefly, the behavioral theory of the firm states that the major functions of theory are to formulate an exhaustive set of general concepts and to specify the critical relationships among system variables. The exhaustive categories in the behavioral theory

[4] Lionel Robbins, *An Essay on the Nature & Significance of Economic Science* (London: Macmillan & Co., Ltd., 1932, reprinted 1952), pp. 94-95.

[5] *Ibid.*, pp. 98-99.

[6] Richard M. Cyert and James G. March, *A Behavioral Theory of the Firm* (Englewood Cliffs, N.J.: Prentice-Hall, Inc., 1963).

are: (1) organizational goals, (2) organizational expectations, and (3) organizational choice. Organizational goals are defined by two sets of variables. The first set relates to the dimensions of goals or identification of matters that are considered important for the operation of the firm. The second set of variables determines the aspiration level for any particular goal dimension.

Organizational expectations are affected primarily by the process through which information is made available. The *nature* of the problem stimulating search activity affects the *direction* of search. The *location* in the organization at which the search is focused also affects the direction of search. The extent to which goals are achieved affects the intensity and effect of search.[7] Organizational choice takes place in response to a presentation of alternatives identified as acceptable in relationship to goals. Organizational choice implies the use of standard operating rules (policies).

In addition to the exhaustive variable categories, four major relational concepts are employed. They are: (1) quasi-resolution of conflict, (2) uncertainty avoidance, (3) problematic search, and (4) organizational learning. The general structure of the organizational decision-making process can be represented as a flow chart in the language of a computer program. The decision process is a continuous closed loop in which the iterative process includes feedback and adjustment mechanisms.[8]

Cyert and March have observed that the conflict between the two theories of the firm in many ways is a false one. The economic theory of the firm is designed to answer a set of questions that have relevance and importance for the operation of an economic system. Important questions about the internal operations of the firm and the processes by which decisions are reached were never intended to be handled by the economic theory of the firm. By focusing on people, organizational motives, and learning theory, the behavioral theory of the firm has been developed to account for significant aspects of the internal operations of the enterprise.

An Historical Perspective [9]

In order to understand fully the implications of the economic and behavioral theories of the firm, it is necessary to place them in proper

---

[7] Organizational slack is defined by Cyert and March. The "difference between total resources and total necessary payments is what we have called *organizational slack*. (Italics theirs.) Slack consists in payments to members of the coalition in excess of what is required to maintain the organization." (*Ibid.*, p. 36.)

[8] Cyert and March, *op. cit.*, p. 125.

[9] The material in this section is based on notes and references developed by Mrs. Sybil Silverman in a course, *History of Science*, presented by Dr. John G. Burke of the Dept. of History, UCLA and on discussions with Dr. Burke and with Dr. Willard F. Libby, Dept. of Chemistry and Geophysics, UCLA.

historical perspective. The economic theory of the firm is a reflection of the Newtonian Revolution of the sixteenth and seventeenth centuries. The behavioral theory of the firm is a reflection of the quantum mechanical and relativistic revolutions of the twentieth century.

Impact of the Newtonian Revolution on Economics

The full impact of the Newtonian Revolution in the physical sciences did not reach the realm of the social sciences until the nineteenth century. The Newtonian Revolution emphasized that there was order in the universe, and the role of the scientist was to discover this order through empirical and theoretical research. From these discoveries the scientist was to deduce rules which applied to specific situations and events.

In economics, the forces of the Newtonian Revolution provided a foundation for the formulation of laws, such as those proposed by Malthus and Ricardo.[10] The laws, like the iron law of wages, were posed as absolutes. The doctrines of laissez-faire economics were also derived from natural law theory. Enunciating this philosophy in his *Wealth of Nations*,[11] Adam Smith proposed that order and harmony could be seen in nature and that natural laws governed the behavior of individuals as well. He reasoned, therefore, that if impersonal, natural forces were able to operate without interference from governmental regulations and restraints, harmony would prevail, and the best interests of society would be served. These doctrines are consonant with the Newtonian Revolution and the application of nature and reason to the social sciences in general and economics in particular.

The Economic Theory of the Firm

The economic theory of the firm postulates the existence of omnipotent laws which govern the behavior of firms in specified environments. These laws are manifested in the impersonal market forces of supply and demand, diminishing returns, etc., and it is also postulated that the firm will seek an equilibrium position. With the emergence of market imperfections, the picture becomes somewhat clouded, but omnipotent laws, with modifications, are still valid.

The implicit, and sometimes explicit, assumption of certainty which is an integral part of the economic theory of the firm stems from the Newtonian concept that there is an order in Nature which is waiting

---

10 Malthus formulated the laws that population tends to grow at a geometric rate of increase while subsistence grows as an arithmetic progression. The iron law of wages is derived from Ricardo. If the wages of the poor are increased, their numbers increase to the level where income per capita again declines to the subsistence level.

11 Adam Smith, *Wealth of Nations* (1776). Available in Everyman's edition.

to be discovered. Thus, the events of the world can be predicted by knowing the structure of this order—which in the economic theory of the firm is the supply and demand conditions, the marginal rates of substitution, etc. Since the behavior of individual firms and industries is determined by the interaction of impersonal market forces, there is no need to deal with the human side of the enterprise, such as the decision-making process, and the problems of organization and control. Thus, the economic theory of the firm emphasizes economic goals and objectives, i.e., profit and/or wealth maximization, rather than the psychologically oriented goals, i.e., satisfaction of expectations and aspirations.

Quantum Mechanics, Relativity, and the Newtonian System

Newtonian laws began to be dismantled in the twentieth century when new phenomena, such as X-rays, gamma rays, radiation, and subatomic particles, could not be explained by reference to the Newtonian system.[12] The possibility of negative gravity, the discovery of increasing numbers of subatomic particles, and the detection of anti-particles continued to restrict the Newtonian universe. A crushing blow was dealt by quantum mechanics, for its theories made intelligible the behavior of these particles and, in demonstrating an increased concern for symmetry, led to the discovery that there are anti-particles for every existing particle in nature. Perhaps, the most important outcome of the quantum mechanical revolution, however, was the destruction of the Newtonian world of certainty by Heisenberg's principle of uncertainty. This principle states that as the certainty about the position of a particle becomes greater, the greater is the uncertainty about its velocity, and vice versa.

In terms of the relativistic revolution, some absolutes of the Newtonian system were discarded, and some parts of the system were combined. The only absolute at the present time is the speed of light, whereas Newton posited absolutes for time and space. Moreover, in Newtonian theory, gravity and electromagnetism were seen as distinct concepts, whereas the relativistic revolution has combined them in the theory of the unified field.

The Behavioral Theory of the Firm

Economics has in the twentieth century undergone a revolution of its own, and the changes made in this field reflect the quantum me-

---

12 The atomic age was launched in 1896 by Henri Becquerel's discovery of the high-energy particles of radioactivity.—*McGraw-Hill Encyclopedia of Science and Technology* (New York: McGraw-Hill Book Company, 1960), III, p. 47.

chanical and relativistic revolutions in the physical sciences. Because there is no natural order which can be discovered, the impersonal market forces of the nineteenth-century economist are not accepted in the behavioral theory of the firm as sufficient to explain the behavior of the business enterprise. The behavioral economist now deals with the decision-making process and with individuals. Thus, the corporate atom has been split, and the presence of uncertainty must be recognized. In this sense, the behavioral theory of the firm is a reflection of the Heisenberg principle of uncertainty. The world of certainty of the nineteenth century has been exchanged for the world of uncertainty in the twentieth.

Since the behavior of individuals is taken to decide the behavior of the business firm ultimately, behavioral theory utilizes the language of psychology, particularly that of learning theory, a field in which a virtual revolution has also taken place. Economics, although not the first to adopt the new, has not been the last to lay the old theories aside, and the paths forged by the pioneers in psychology have laid down the foundation of the behavioral theory of the firm.

The behavioral theory of the firm represents the application of one school of learning psychology in particular. Its characteristics may be clarified by summarizing the other major approaches to learning. In classical Pavlovian conditioning theory, a conditioned (learned) stimulus will elicit a response by being paired with an unconditioned (unlearned) stimulus which already elicits the response. The reinforcement appears after the response is elicited. For example, the dog salivates (responds) when food (stimulus) is presented; the reinforcement is eating. Through conditioning, the dog learns to salivate (conditioned response) to a bell (conditioned stimulus). Again, the reinforcement is eating.

A second type of learning is instrumental which is attributed to Thorndike. In this type of conditioning, the reinforcement is the goal from the very beginning and provides the stimulus for the response. For example, a pigeon in a box sees a black button. Through trial and error, it discovers that when the button is pushed, food appears. Thus, the button is the stimulus for the response (pushing the button) for which the pigeon receives the reinforcement of food. Thus, the pigeon learns to push the button.

The behavioral theory of learning concentrates on the "human," "individual," aspects of learning. Learning is not just a series of stimuli and responses but rather responses of a complex organism to a complex situation. For example, behaviorists would find that a child's learning to read greatly depends upon his motivation, his level of aspiration. Does he want to read? Will fear of failure stop the child from learning, indicating a low level of aspiration? In the behavioral theory of the firm, the process is similar. The focus is on how goals are set, decisions made, and upon how decisions are implemented. The analysis of organizational expectation is similar to the analysis of the level of aspiration.

The behavioral economist, therefore, does not deal with impersonal market forces but with individuals. The organization processes determine the policies which are carried out by the operating executives and managers in directing the behavior of the enterprise. The focus is not upon economic objectives of profit and/or wealth maximization but upon the attainment of social and psychological objectives and the satisfaction of expectations within the context of organization goals, expectations, and choice.

The communication of information in the decision-making process attains paramount importance in the behavioral theory of the firm, because it is necessary for each individual to be cognizant of organizational goals and aspirations in order to promote the achievement of those objectives through the search process. The individuals responsible for directing the corporation learn the procedures for direction through both formal schooling and actual experience. Thus, formal schooling is comparable to heredity in psychology; it is the background with which the individual comes into the corporate world. The successes and failures resulting from the decisions of the corporate executives play the role of reward and punishment in learning theory.

The behavioral theory of the firm is a reflection of both the quantum mechanical and relativistic revolutions in the physical sciences. The quantum mechanical aspect has been discussed in relation to the application of psychology to the behavior of the enterprise. The relativistic revolution may be seen in the rejection of absolutes in favor of interrelationships. For example, the heretofore distinct functional areas of management, such as production, marketing, and finance, have become blurred. In addition, its reverberations may be seen in the recognition of the relationship between sociology, psychology, and the theory of the firm which has culminated in the behavioral theory of the firm. Once, the enterprise was considered to be solely in the realm of classical economics. Thus, both the operation of the firm and the economics which attempts to explain and predict the behavior of the enterprise have been broadened. New symmetries and relationships have been sought, recognized, and explored by behavioral economists.

The Nature of Theory

Another set of building blocks is necessary for the discussion of the finance function which follows in subsequent chapters. These building blocks may be subsumed under the general title, "The Nature of Theory."

The Axiomatic Method

The nature of theory is derived from the use of "The Axiomatic Method." [13] "In Euclidian geometry, axioms were self-evident truths," and postulates were plausible truths derived from the axioms. From the axioms and postulates, 465 propositions could be deduced in a logical chain.[14] The modern axiomatic method starts with certain basic statements called axioms (or postulates) which are assumptions regarded as plausible for the universe of discourse, i.e., the subject under discussion. The axioms are "primary propositions" to be left unproved in the system.[15] In addition to the axioms, certain undefined technical terms as well as the operations of classical logic are added. With the assumptions (axioms) and the basic terms (which are undefined in the axiomatic method), propositions can be developed by a system of logical deduction.

The distinction between axioms in Euclidian geometry and axioms in modern mathematical methodology may be briefly illustrated. In Euclidian geometry, it was taken as an axiom that a straight line was the shortest distance between two points. For the universe of discourse under the assumption of flat surfaces, this is valid. On a sphere, the great circle is the shortest distance between two points. This example illustrates that self-evident truths are convenient assumptions for the universe of discourse chosen. Propositions are statements derived by logical operations from the axioms or postulates plus the definitions. Propositions have truth value in the sense that they can be tested. In pure theory or in pure mathematical systems, the test of a proposition is internal consistency with the model. There is no attempt to match the propositions to the real world.

In this connection a dispute over the role of assumptions has arisen. Professor Friedman has stated that the realism of assumptions is no test of the validity of a hypothesis. He presents the following example:

> Consider the problem of predicting the shots made by an expert billiard player. It seems not at all unreasonable that excellent predictions would be yielded by the hypothesis that the billiard player made his shots *as if* he knew the complicated mathematical formulas that would give the optimum directions of travel, could estimate accurately by eye the angles, etc., describing the location of the balls, could make lightning calculations from the formulas, and could then make the balls travel in the direction indicated by the formulas. Our confidence in this hypothesis is not based on the belief that billiard players, even

---

13 See, for example, Raymond L. Wilder, *Introduction to the Foundations of Mathematics* (New York: John Wiley & Sons, Inc., 1952), pp. 3-49.

14 *Ibid.*, p. 4.

15 *Ibid.*, p. 10.

expert ones, can or do go through the process described; it derives rather from the belief that, unless in some way or other they were capable of reaching essentially the same result, they would not, in fact, be *expert* billiard players.[16]

This position has been disputed. A distinction is drawn between prediction and explanation. Cohen and Cyert have summarized the objection as follows:

> Friedman's position may lead to prediction without explanation. Referring again to the billiard player example, . . . the model has no explanatory power. Any predictive power that the model may have would arise from some unknown relationship between variables in the model and some unknown variables not included in the model. If our scientific standards require a model which can provide explanation as well as prediction, then the billiard player model is unsatisfactory.[17]

There is validity in both views. Friedman's analogy is somewhat misleading from the standpoint of the basic position he was seeking to explain. In his original presentation he immediately moved to an economic application. In predicting and explaining the operation of an economic system, a model of the behavior of individual firms can be constructed in which marginal cost is equated to marginal revenues. The consequences of a change in demand or cost conditions will lead to predictable consequences. It is not that the large system of simultaneous equations of the marketplace are solved by the businessman. He receives a continuing stream of information which tells him of the effects of his decisions and leads to a continuous sequential information adjustment process. In this sense, economic theory both predicts and explains in terms of its own universe of discourse.

Another approach to prediction is represented by modern control theory. Modern control theory focuses on inputs into "black boxes" and their outputs. The "black box" refers to a transformation process whose operations are not fully observable or understood. But stability of relations between inputs into partially controlled environments and resulting outputs provides a basis for devising systems that are operationally effective. The operation of the system is predictable, based on unknown but dependable order in the universe.

The development of modern control theory reinforces the Friedman approach to the development of theory. It does not seek to obtain an understanding of the transformation processes, goals, aspira-

---

16 Milton Friedman, "The Methodology of Positive Economics," *Essays in Positive Economics* (Chicago: The University of Chicago Press, 1953), p. 21.

17 Kalman J. Cohen and Richard M. Cyert, *Theory of the Firm: Resource Allocation in a Market Economy* (Englewood Cliffs, N.J.: Prentice-Hall, Inc., 1965), p. 24. See also: R. M. Cyert and E. Grunberg, "Assumption, Prediction, and Explanation in Economics," Appendix A in Richard M. Cyert and James G. March, *A Behavioral Theory of the Firm* (Englewood Cliffs, N.J.: Prentice-Hall, Inc., 1963), 298-311.

tions, etc. But it simply focuses on understanding a pattern of stability relationships between inputs and outputs.

But the essential issue is not the nature of assumptions but the nature of the world. The naturalist position held that basic laws governed the behavior of the universe in a deterministic way. The rejection of natural laws led to a relativistic position and implies that man may alter and control elements of his environment.

The important point about explanation is not explanation itself. It is control. The reason we cannot accept the purist position that prediction is the end of science is because man chooses to alter his environment. He seeks explanation for control or policy purposes so he can influence outcomes and not as an end in itself. The evolution of the axiomatic method changes it from a deterministic to a relativistic position. It becomes a method for helping man understand and control his environment.

The Methodology of Research

A number of theories might be consistent with a given set of data. Thus, to assert that a particular theory has been applied to some facts and that the facts "confirm the theory" is an overstatement. If a theory is tested by reference to some empirical data, it is more accurate to say that data or facts are consistent with the theory. The data may also be consistent with other theories. Thus, a theory is not "proved" by a set of facts. Our degree of confidence in the theory is increased by showing that it is consistent with a particular set of facts.

This distinction may be clarified by a brief summary of the sharp cleavage in approaches to testing business cycle theories in economics. One approach represented by the National Bureau of Economic Research was essentially empirical in its orientation. By examining a large body of factual material, it was hoped that foundations for formulating some generalizations might be achieved. This approach was criticized by the Cowles Commission which expressed a point of view most strongly set forth by Professor Koopmans in his review of Burns and Mitchell, *Measuring Business Cycles* (1946).[18] Koopmans observes,

> . . . even for the purpose of systematic and large scale observation of such a many sided phenomenon, theoretical preconceptions about its nature cannot be dispensed with and the authors do so only to the detriment of the analysis.[19]

On the other hand, the explanations for the empirical approach have been set forth effectively by their intellectual father, Wesley Clair Mitchell, in a letter of August 9, 1928 to John Maurice Clark.

---

[18] Tjalling C. Koopmans, "Measurement Without Theory," *The Review of Economics and Statistics*, XXIX (August, 1947), 161-72.

[19] *Ibid.*, p. 163.

I began studying philosophy and economics about the same time. The similarity of the two disciplines struck me at once. I found no difficulty in grasping the differences between the great philosophical systems as they were presented by our textbooks and our teachers. Economic theory was easier still. Indeed, I thought the successive systems of economics were rather crude affairs compared with the subtleties of the metaphysicians. Having run the gamut from Plato to T. H. Green (as undergraduates do) I felt the gamut from Quesnay to Marshall was a minor theme. The technical part of the theory was easy. *Give me premises and I could spin speculations by the yard. Also I knew that my "deductions" were futile.* It seemed to me that people who took seriously the sort of articles which were then appearing in the Q.J.E. might have a better time if they went in for metaphysics proper.[20]

The point of view which Mitchell expressed was that premises or assumptions could be multiplied without end. One could, therefore, generate an infinite number of propositions to be tested. Hence, Mitchell suggested that economists look at the real world, describe it in primitive terms, and then use the description as a basis for formulating some assumptions or premises that could be developed into propositions. The answer of the Cowles Commission is that without some theoretical preconceptions one has no basis for determining what things shall be described. Therefore, on the basis of some theoretical preconceptions, one begins by testing propositions developed from some plausible assumptions. This approach requires a basis for plausible theory. Each approach faces a dilemma, though, clearly, each approach has its usefulness. What is required is a tentative formulation of assumptions and a development of propositions. These provide a basis for gathering data to observe consistency of empirical data with propositions. In turn, such descriptive data may require a modification in assumptions, which in turn stimulates additional kinds of empirical inquiries for testing the new propositions.

A clear illustration from the finance field of the modern theoretical approach is provided in the now famous Modigliani-Miller article.[21] The Modigliani and Miller article formulated some assumptions based on attitudes of investors toward risk and some fundamental assumptions of economic theory. To these assumptions they added some related definitions, and with the assumptions and definitions, they developed some propositions. They then tested the propositions by empirical studies and found that the data in the empirical studies

20 From a letter quoted in Lucy Sprague Mitchell, "A Personal Sketch," in *Wesley Clair Mitchell, The Economic Scientist,* Arthur F. Burns (ed.) (New York: National Bureau of Economic Research, Inc., 1952), pp. 94-95.

21 Franco Modigliani and Merton H. Miller, "The Cost of Capital Corporation Finance, and the Theory of Investments," *The American Economic Review,* June, 1958, pp. 261-96.

were consistent with the propositions which they derived from their assumptions.

The Modigliani-Miller theory cannot be evaluated by arguing with the reasonableness of their assumptions as some of their critics have done. Any set of assumptions that is plausible can be used. There is no way of settling *a priori* whether one set of assumptions may be better than any other set of assumptions. There is a free market in assumptions.

The evaluation of propositions has to be achieved by examining the soundness of their empirical tests or repeating their empirical tests to determine whether similar results are obtained. If empirical tests are repeated and the same results are obtained, the plausibility of the assumptions and the validity of the theories developed from the assumption could be placed on a higher level of credibility. If subsequent empirical tests turn up results that are inconsistent with their propositions, then serious doubt may be cast on their basic assumptions.

Only after empirical tests are repeated and give results that are different from those predicted by propositions derived from the Modigliani-Miller assumptions is one justified in questioning the validity of their assumptions. In this connection, in my own iteration of tests of their propositions by empirical studies, I observed results different from their results.[22] If subsequent empirical studies turn up different results, then the Modigliani and Miller assumptions may properly be questioned. Other assumptions may therefore be substituted. Alternative propositions are generated and tested by repeated empirical studies.

In this monograph, *theories* will be regarded as synonymous with propositions. Propositions or theories are relationships deduced from fundamental axioms and definitions and, at the theoretical level, are testable only for their internal consistency with the axioms and definitions of the system. For use in decision-making, they must be tested for their ability to predict or explain empirical data. Principles may be defined as propositions or theories which have been found to be consistent with empirical data.

Positive vs. Normative Theory

The foregoing discussion suggests another dimension of theories, i.e., the distinction between positive or descriptive theory and normative or prescriptive theory. Positive theory seeks to describe and understand how the object of the study or description behaves. To describe is to help understand. The subject may be mice in a maze, or it may be businessmen making capital budgeting decisions.

22 J. Fred Weston, "A Test of Cost of Capital Propositions," *The Southern Economics Journal,* XXX (October, 1963), 105-12.

But what businessmen or mice *are* doing may be different from what they *ought* to be doing. Here, we are dealing with normative or prescriptive theory. The scientist may perceive that there are more efficient ways and less efficient ways for an animal to tread a maze. In this sense the scientists may teach mice how to behave more efficiently. On the other hand, if the researcher is seeking to understand something fundamental about the psychology of mice or related organisms or the nature of learning theory under elementary circumstances, he may seek only a descriptive theory.

Similarly, in a theory of the firm, or in capital budgeting, we may be seeking to understand how a businessman makes his decisions. We may observe that a two-to-three-year cash payout is the fundamental investment hurdle that is used by businessmen. But, as economists, we may argue that a two-to-three-year cash payback investment hurdle is undesirable from the standpoint of both the firm and the economy. We may argue that it results in an implicit cost of capital that is so high that it restricts the rate of investment. We may argue that it results in a capital formation rate that slows down the growth of the economy and limits the profitability of the firm. We may, therefore, turn to a normative or prescriptive theory and tell businessmen how they ought to behave in connection with capital budgeting decisions. We may formulate capital expenditure decision rules consistent with the psychology of learning, with fundamental economic propositions, and with business cycle theory. Such prescriptive theory is formulated to tell businessmen how they ought to behave.

It is important in the development of propositions in business or in economics to separate descriptive and prescriptive propositions. There is a danger in mixing positive and normative approaches in developing theories that may be inaccurate descriptions of the real world or unsound guides to policy for businessmen because of their lack of proper relationship to the conditions of the real world. A clear understanding, therefore, of the nature of theory and of propositions is necessary. Many policy statements and policy recommendations in a firm, or wherever decisions are being made, are in the nature of propositions. Their validity can be tested. But such statements are often regarded as self-evident truths or based on assumptions about the nature of the real world that have no validity. The propositions or theories for the guidance of business firms are equally subject to testing as the propositions and theories of the operation and behavior of the economic system as a whole.

In connection with the discussion of the formulation of propositions for the guidance of business behavior, some other concepts may usefully be defined. It should be clear from the previous discussion of the nature of modern methodology that definitions are inherently arbitrary. Definitions are arbitrary statements that may be justified because of their convenience in providing a language for carrying on a discussion. Thus, the description of modern mathematical theory or modern methodology is arbitrary in itself. Other methodologies could likewise be defined. The argument in support of the methodology that has been recommended by this presentation is that it has internal consistency and it is consistent with a large body of logical methodology. It draws on a long history of logical methodology refined only by recognizing the inherent arbitrariness of some of the fundamental relationships upon which the logical systems are developed.

One fundamental task of methodologies is pragmatic.[23] Which set of methodologies results in propositions that provide useful guidance for the decision-maker? Even this test is not a conclusive one, however. Many mathematical systems have been developed in recent years as exercises in pure theory. Their justification was only the strong drive of the theorist for examining the logical consequences of different kinds of pure mathematical systems. But ironically, some of the pure mathematical systems have turned out to have great practical applications. Pure theory has found application in modern developments in physics, chemistry, and in astrophysics. Some "pure" systems have found application in the explorations of space where the underlying physical conditions and, therefore, appropriate assumptions about the nature of physics and chemistry are fundamentally different from conditions on the earth.

This wide-ranging methodological discourse may seem a digression. But given the dynamic nature of the environment in which business decisions, including financial decisions, are made, it appears imperative to understand clearly the inherently arbitrary nature of much of what is accepted as well-established.

In contrast to the older finance materials preoccupied with descriptions of instruments and institutions, the newer studies in finance bring to its subject matter a theory or a framework of propositions. When instruments, institutions, or empirical materials are examined within a theory, the focus of analysis is sharpened. The materials developed either confirm or deny a hypothesis. The development of a body of tested doctrine is, thereby, made possible. Difficult problems will remain difficult and may not be solved for decades. But progress will be enhanced if the empirical data and descriptive materials are relevant to a theoretical framework. Indeed, without such a framework, we are likely to be overwhelmed by the sheer accumulation of the masses of materials.

It is in this connection that Professors Franco Modigliani and Merton H. Miller have made a lasting contribution to the field of finance. Regardless of whether subsequent empirical studies support or deny their propositions about the influence of leverage and dividend policy on business valuation, they have formulated some basic hy-

---

[23] An equally justifiable rationale for methodology is pure intellectual curiosity.

potheses that represent a valuable framework for approaching materials in the field of finance.

The Role of Models in Analytical Studies

A background has been established for a discussion of models as instruments for formulating and testing theories. A model is a representation of reality by its main properties.[24] The essentials of reality are expressed in symbolic form. Different types of models have been classified by different writers. One distinguishes three types: deterministic, stochastic, and game models.[25] In the deterministic models the variables are under control of the decision-makers. A stochastic model is based on probabilities when the values in the model are subject to random variations. The game model is employed when the results of a decision or action depend on the behavior of opponents.

An illuminating discussion of the nature and use of models is provided by Ackoff and Rivett.[26] They state that a model relates controlled variables (C) and uncontrolled variables (U) to performance (P). Thus, in formal terms:

$$P = f(C,U)$$

The basic model may be supplemented by statements which reflect limitations on possible values of the controlled variables. These are constraints. The solution to the model consists of determining the values of controllable variables which maximize performance (this may involve minimizing costs). The solution may be extracted by mathematical analysis and other techniques which will be discussed below. The solutions consist of one equation for each controllable variable. The optimizing values of the controlled variables are expressed as functions of the values of the uncontrolled variables. These equations are called "decision rules." [27]

Some distinctions may be drawn between the terms that have been introduced. *Definitions* provide a language for analysis. *Models* represent a method of analysis to evaluate alternative courses of action and to provide a basis for executive decisions. *Policies* represent a guide to executive decisions that will contribute to progress

[24] Kalman J. Cohen and Richard M. Cyert, *Theory of the Firm* (Englewood Cliffs, N.J.: Prentice-Hall, Inc., 1965), pp. 18-28.

[25] Martin Zober, *Marketing Management* (New York: John Wiley & Sons, Inc., 1964), pp. 301-2.

[26] Russell L. Ackoff and Patrick Rivett, *A Manager's Guide to Operations Research* (New York: John Wiley & Sons, Inc., 1963), pp. 27-29.

[27] *Ibid.*, p. 28.

toward enterprise goals. Definitions are arbitrary but useful in providing a language. Policies are formulated in areas that affect the performance of the enterprise. Models are constructed for the purpose of improving policies and decisions. Thus, definitions and models provide useful tools for analytical study of alternatives to improve decisions. The resulting process represents a scientific approach to management problems. The aim is to improve policies to contribute to optimizing behavior.

Optimal is a term that has meaning only within the context of the model. If the model is inapplicable, the "optimum" may be a very bad solution to the problem. Hence the testing of normative models while difficult, becomes of great importance.

Forecasting, Projecting, and Budgeting

An important area of decision-making involves the future consequences of present decisions or activities. Other related concepts are defined in connection with the future. The nature of the world consists of present acts, followed by subsequent consequences. Every set of events in the real world may be defined as a *system*. A system may be defined as a set of cause-and-effect relationships. The three major parts consist of inputs (I), a transformation function (T), and outputs (O). Another set of distinctions may, therefore, be formulated in connection with the behavior of a system. To *project* or make a projection is to take given *assumed values* of I and T to describe O. Alternative sets of I's and T's could be employed to describe alternative sets of O's. *Forecasts* represent probability statements about I and T to permit probability statements about O, subject to revision with increased information. In connection with setting a target or targets, the inputs or structure can be periodically altered or controlled to achieve a specified O or a range of O. Planning represents a formulation of alternative sets of I's and T's with related outputs. To plan is to select among alternatives covering a period of time longer than one year with related resource allocations to achieve long-range targets. To *program* is to allocate resources within a plan for achieving short-run targets. A *budget* is a type of program representing an allocation of resources within a plan for achieving short-term targets. A budget represents a resource allocation device.

The degree of our knowledge about future events suggests additional distinctions. One writer has set out the following classification which is generally consistent with the dominant stream of literature in this area.[28]

---

[28] H. Igor Ansoff, *Corporate Strategy* (New York: McGraw-Hill Book Company, 1965), pp. 118-21.

Degree of Knowledge of the Future	*Class of Loss Exposure*
1. Alternatives are known	
2. Probabilities assigned to outcomes	RISK
1. Alternatives are known	
2. Probabilities of outcomes not known	UNCERTAINTY
1. Alternatives are not known	
2. Probabilities of outcomes not known	PARTIAL IGNORANCE

In problems involving risk, stochastic models may be employed because probabilities are known or can be assigned to alternative outcomes. Under uncertainty, the alternatives are known, but probabilities cannot be assigned to the alternative outcomes or their values. Policies are formulated to deal with uncertainty situations. The policies provide guides to executive decisions, but the actuarial value of outcomes cannot be specified because probabilities cannot be assigned to alternatives.[29] Where neither alternatives nor the probabilities of outcomes cannot be formulated, ignorance or partial ignorance exists. Policies under partial ignorance are sometimes referred to as a strategy, defined as rules for decision under partial ignorance.[30]

The Methodology of Management Science

The foregoing discussion of risk, uncertainty, and partial ignorance suggests a distinction between two basic types of problems. One type may be termed well-structured problems. These are problems for which the data are repetitive or for which probabilities may be assigned to outcomes to constitute stochastic problems. Other types of problems involve uncertainty or partial ignorance. To date, management science has dealt primarily with well-structured problems but is beginning to progress toward handling the ill-structured problems.

Basic Types of Management Problems

Ackoff and Rivett have summarized management science problems into a limited number of basic types.

> . . . [We] put forward the following eight basic forms, which singly or in combination account for most of the problems that confront executives. . . . The classification of problems is:

---

[29] An intermediate case is represented by assigning subjective probabilities and applying decision theory. See, for example, C. J. Grayson, *Decisions Under Uncertainty* (Boston: Division of Research, Harvard Business School, 1960); R. Duncan Luce, and Howard Raiffa, *Games and Decisions* (New York: John Wiley & Sons, Inc., 1957); Howard Raiffa and Robert Schlaifer, *Applied Statistical Decision Theory* (Boston: Division of Research, Harvard Business School, 1961).

[30] Ansoff, *op. cit.*, p. 120.

1. Inventory
2. Allocation
3. Queuing
4. Sequencing
5. Routing
6. Replacement
7. Search
8. Competition [31]

In their discussion, they describe the nature of the problems and the basic methodologies to be used in solving them. These are summarized in Table 3-1, which is best understood in terms of the following reformulation which summarizes the relations between the eight classes of problems outlined by Ackoff and Rivett. I have regrouped the eight types of problems into four types.

Table 3-1: The Methodology of Management Science

Form and Content of the Problem	Solution to be Provided	Techniques to be Employed
I. Inventory How much idle resources to hold? Quantity and timing of purchases Two types of costs: one that increases with inventories; one that decreases with inventories	Two principal types of costs: Increase with inventory size: 1. Storage Decrease with inventory size: 1. Shortage 2. Setup and takedown costs 3. Purchase or production costs 4. Labor stabilization costs	Programming Calculus Simulation
II. Allocation 	$R < J$ Budgeting $R > J$ Diversification $R = J$ Plant Location	Programming Simulation
III. Queuing 	Rules for waiting by Customers Schedule Customers Control Facilities available	Programming Simulation

---

[31] Russell L. Ackoff and Patrick Rivett, "The Form and Content of Problems," *A Manager's Guide to Operations Research* (New York: John Wiley & Sons, Inc., 1963), pp. 34-61.

Table 3-1: The Methodology of Management Science (Cont.)

Form and Content of the Problem	Solution to be Provided	Techniques to be Employed
IV. Sequencing	Select a queue to minimize some measure of performance PERT CPM	Same as Queuing
V. Network Problems 　Sequence—minimum 　　time 　Network—minimize cost	Go through a sequence of places to minimize cost, time, distance, capacity limits	Same as Queuing
VI. Replacement Decisions 　1. Degenerating assets 　　a. efficiency decreases 　　　with time or use 　　b. large and expensive 　　　(plant and equip- 　　　ment)	Cost of maintenance and lost efficiency vs. cost of capital	Dynamic Programming
2. Nondegenerative 　　a. wear out all at once 　　b. unit cost is small 　　　(light bulbs)	Replace all at fixed intervals and individually as fail	
VII. Search Problems	Sampling error—failure to detect because inadequate coverage	Sampling Theory
	Observational errors—failure to detect even though looked	Decision Theory
VIII. Competitive Problems 　What will rivals do?	Actions and reactions of rivals	Game Theory Decision Theory

In Group I, three similar types of problems are included. These are: (1) Inventory, (2) Replacement, (3) Search problems (sampling). These three have some characteristics in common. For each, some costs go down, and some rise with quantity. In inventory problems, storage costs increase with the size of inventory holdings, while shortage or outage costs decrease with the size of inventory holdings. In replacement decisions, the costs of maintenance and lost efficiency rise with the age of equipment, but capital costs increase, if replacement is sooner. In search problems, the costs of observations rise with greater coverage, but sampling error costs rise with less coverage.

For the combination of costs, therefore, there is a declining and a rising segment. For cost control, management science seeks to find the range of minimum costs. This is achieved by programming and simulation studies.

I would also group the following three types of problems: (1) Queuing, (2) Sequencing, (3) Network. These all involve decision

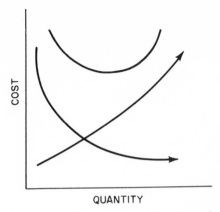

Figure 3-1.   Cost Patterns in Inventory-Type Problems

rules for waiting and movement through a service facility. The object is to achieve queuing rules for minimizing time and cost, and programming and simulation techniques are employed.

The third type of problem is the allocation problem. We have a matrix of *Jobs* to be performed and a set of types of *Resources* for performing the jobs. Basically, a location and sequencing problem is likely to be involved. When resources are exceeded by the jobs to be performed, we have a budgeting problem. Budgeting allocates limited resources to competing uses. When resources exceed the number of jobs to be done, the firm has an idle resources problem. It faces the problem of finding additional uses for its resources—this is the diversification problem.

Finally, the fourth set of problems is competitive problems. These are created by the uncertain and changing environment and by the actions and reactions of competitors (rivals). The problems are attacked by the methods of decision theory and game theory.

The vast complexity of problems becomes more manageable when viewed as one of a special case of a broader class of problems. The framework provided by the management science studies is of great value in achieving improved understanding of methods for handling business problems. The tools of management science do not preclude the use of search methods for defining and formulating business problems.

Classes of Business Finance Problems

It may provide a useful perspective to assess the nature of business finance problems and decisions within the framework of the categories explained above. The issues of business finance concerned with asset management, including fund flow analysis, are basically inventory and replacement-type problems. Clearly, the asset investment decisions are all inventory-type decisions. The plant and equipment or fixed asset decisions are different in that increased maintenance and loss-in-efficiency costs rise with age.

Turning to the right hand side of the balance sheet, we confront the financing mix problems. Choice of financing mix is a leverage problem comparable to the degree of specialization chosen for fixed assets. If fixed-return instruments are employed, a firm with favorable returns on assets will benefit from leverage up to a range of debt-to-equity ratios. As the cost of capital functions rise, a range is reached in which the gains from substituting the lower cost sources of financing for the higher will cause the capitalization rates to rise to the point where the value of the firm passes its maximum and begins to decline. We thus have a type of inventory-problem wherein some cost elements are rising and others are falling. This implies a U-shaped cost function. The aim is to find the financing mix with results that correspond to the lower cost range.

Another major decision-area for finance is the choice of liquidity levels. Liquidity problems have a close correspondence to queuing theory problems. Less liquidity results in greater profitability and corresponds to fewer check-out stands and clerks in a supermarket. Too much waiting-in-line at a given store might cause customers to shift to another store where the waiting period is shorter, but the store's costs are, therefore, higher. Less liquidity results in greater profitability, but an illiquid position may result in bankruptcy or inability to seize favorable opportunities.

Diversification, mergers, and strategies for growth are partly financial problems and partly other types of management problems. They clearly involve the basic problems of search, allocation, and the competitive problems. These are types of areas whose nature is more akin to the ill-structured problems described in the next section.

Uncertainty and Ill-Structured Problems

In contrast to the well-structured problems that lend themselves to treatment by developed management-science methods, there are the decisions that must be made under uncertainty.[32] These are the ill-structured problems of business policy. These are the kinds of problems for which the parameters of the probability distributions associated with future outcomes are not known. These are problems such as: What are the sales going to be in this particular industry over the next ten years? Are special purpose computers going to grow faster in sales than general purpose computers? Or, does the firm that makes

---

[32] Ansoff, *op. cit.*, pp. 172-206.

office copying equipment have the same kind of growth potential that IBM had in large-scale computers? How much significance does the price of entry have, the number of years that one of these firms will be relatively free from sales to capacity problems, in their line of business?

These kinds of ill-structured problems require a different method of solution which is iterative in nature. It requires repeated "closing the loop" in the following decision steps:

1. State the firm's objectives.
2. Define the nature of the firm's environment.
3. Evaluate the firm's strengths and weaknesses in relation to its environment.
4. Assess the firm's potential in its environment.
5. Compare the potential with the firm's objectives.
6. If a gap exists, search for alternatives for closing the gap between potential and objectives.
7. Select alternatives for analysis.
8. The benefits and costs of alternative policies are calculated.
9. A tentative selection from among alternatives is made (i.e., a plan is formulated).
10. The process is repeated to check the conclusions reached. Sometimes the process is gone through first from a research standpoint, from a production standpoint, from a marketing standpoint, from a financial standpoint, and finally from an over-all enterprise or systems approach.
11. Resources are committed to implement a plan.
12. A follow-up is performed to compare performance with plan.
13. The comparison of objectives and prospects is repeated.

When it is necessary to take action to close a prospective gap between the firm's objectives and its potential based on its present capabilities, some soul-searching choices must be made. Shall the firm attempt to change its environment or capabilities? What will be the costs of such changes? What are the risks and unknowns? What are the rewards if successful? What are the penalties of failure? Because the stakes are large, the iterative process is employed. A tentative decision is made. The process is repeated, perhaps from a different management function orientation. At some point, the total enterprise point of view is brought to bear on the problem. At some point, decisions are made and must involve entrepreneurial judgments.

Chapter Summary

This chapter began by contrasting the approaches of the economic theory of the firm and of the behavioral theory of the firm for describing and prescribing business policy in general and financial policy in particular. The economic theory of the firm is in the Newtonian and natural law doctrines of the sixteenth and seventeenth centuries which saw order in nature independent of the behavior of individuals or individual atoms. In contrast, the behavioral theory of the firm reflects the emphasis of the relativistic revolution in which Newtonian absolutes are modified. It reflects the emphasis of the field of psychology on individual differences, on learning theory, on social and psychological objectives, on the satisfaction of expectations and aspirations within the framework of organization goals, expectations, and choice.

At least in part these differences in approach reflect differences in the types of problems studied. Economics and sociology may make generalizations about the behavior of groups which may ignore individual differences. Psychology and behavioral theory emphasize the interaction of individuals in groups in studying group processes. As Cyert and March have observed, analysis of the operation of the economic system requires an approach different from that which studies the internal operations of the firm and the processes by which decisions are reached. The two types of problems are interrelated at some points when behavioral relations for the system as a whole are formulated. The differences in approaches are critical for understanding the nature of theory. Theories are developed from assumptions and definitions which are used to formulate systems and propositions. Critical in the development of theories is the nature of the assumptions upon which the structure of the system is based. Pure systems yield propositions or theories that can be tested for their internal consistency.

For policy areas, an additional test is applied. Does the theory explain or predict the real world? The actual world is so complex and filled with detail that its bewildering immensity and diversity must be reduced in order to begin to comprehend it. Models perform the useful function of reducing reality to its main properties. To have a basis for beginning to approach reality by measurement and description, initial guidance is provided by theories. But the theories in turn were based on assumptions which appeared plausible for the universe of discourse. Thus a theory is based on some initial experience with reality and description is based on some prior formulation of theories. The necessity of an iterative process is clear.

In formulating models, the relationship between controlled variables is stable; the problems are well-structured. They yield to the methods of management science. When the outcomes of occurrences involve substantial unknowns, we face uncertainty or partial ignorance. The methods of search and iterated review and analysis of the objectives, potentials, alternatives, benefits and costs must be employed.

The methods of the economic theory of the firm and of the behavioral theory of the firm are not competitive, but complementary. Each is powerful for some classes of problems. Similarly, the methodology for handling well-structured problems and for handling ill-structured problems overlap and may reinforce each other. These different approaches have the common goal of improving theory and policies. To illustrate their application in the field of finance is the function of the following chapters.

In Chapter 4 which follows, some aspects of the organization structure of the business firm will be treated. In Chapter 5, the scope of the finance function and financial policy will be discussed.

```
44444444444444444444444444444444444444444444444444444444444444444444444444444444
44444444444444444444444444444444444444444444444444444444444444444444444444444444
4444444444444444444444444444444   444   4444.44444444    44444444444444444444444444
4444444444444444444444444444444   4444   44444444444   44444444444444444444444444
4444444444444444444444444444444   44444   444444444   44444444444444444444444444
4444444444444444444444444444444   444444   4444444   44444444444444444444444444
4444444444444444444444444444444   4444444   44444   44444444444444444444444444
4444444444444444444444444444444   44444444   444   44444444444444444444444444
4444444444444444444444444444444   444444444   4   44444444444444444444444444
4444444444444444444444444444444   4444444444   44444444444444444444444444444
4444444444444444444444444444444   44444444444   44444444444444444444444444444
44444444444444444444444444444444444444444444444444444444444444444444444444444444
44444444444444444444444444444444444444444444444444444444444444444444444444444444
```

The Finance Function in the Organization Framework

IN THIS chapter, the financial activities of the firm are viewed from the perspective of organizational relationships and processes. Initially, the objective was to attempt an analysis of the finance function in the framework of a rigorous behavioral theory of the firm. A promising beginning has been achieved for segments of the activities of financial institutions.[1] It would provide valuable insights and understanding if the subject matter could be developed in terms of organization goals, expectations, and choice. The material could also be discussed in terms of the four major relational concepts of behavioral theory in terms of: (1) quasi-resolution of conflict, (2) uncertainty avoidance, (3) problem search, and (4) organizational learning. The traditional material has, however, never been systematically brought together. To provide a basis for a comparison of the understanding achieved by the traditional approach and the newer behavioral theory, it will be useful to present and systemize the existing literature. Hence, this presentation of the finance function will be in the framework of neo-classical organization and management theory. Hopefully, at some future date,

---

[1] G. P. E. Clarkson, *Portfolio Selection: A Simulation of Trust Investment* (Englewood Cliffs, N.J.: Prentice-Hall, Inc., 1962); See also, R. M. Cyert and J. G. March, *A Behavioral Theory of the Firm* (Englewood Cliffs, N.J.: Prentice-Hall, Inc., 1963), pp. 253-67.

others trained in the behavioral approach will reflect on these materials and attempt to compare and contrast them to the behavioral framework.

The Basic Approach

In beginning an analysis of the finance function, a fundamental choice is presented. Shall we proceed by developing a normative theory of the finance function or a descriptive theory? Writers sometimes discuss the finance function as though there were a normative theory of the finance function. Usually such a normative theory emphasizes that the main responsibility of finance is in connection with fund movements. It is argued that other functionaries in the firm are responsible for the design, manufacture, and sale of products. Such a description of the finance function breaks down upon further analysis. Is finance responsible only for the acquisition of funds, or for following through their utilization in the firm? It can be viewed as responsible for the effective utilization of funds, but it is difficult to separate analysis of funds movements and analysis of related operations in the firm with which the fund movements are associated. Furthermore, other writers apparently proceeding from a normative approach argue that finance has responsibilities beyond fund movements. For example, Ezra Solomon in an analytical treatment of financial management concludes:

> If the scope of financial management is redefined to cover decisions about both the use and the acquisition of funds, it is clear that the principal content of the subject should be concerned with how financial management should make judgments about whether an enterprise should hold, reduce, or increase its investment in all forms of assets that require company funds.[2]

The central issue here is: Can investment decisions of the firm be made independently of financial decisions? Some writers develop their analysis as though financial decisions are made without regard to the nature of the objectives and investment opportunities of the firm. The position that will be taken in this study is that investment decisions are inextricably related to financial decisions.

In Professor Solomon's formulation of the finance function, the emphasis is on resource allocation as well as fund allocation. He points out that the approach he describes requires the following prerequisites:

1. The establishment of an explicit goal, such as maximization of the present worth of the ownership.

---

2 Ezra Solomon, *The Theory of Financial Management* (New York: Columbia University Press, 1963), p. 8.

2. Organizational framework such as relevant information. This includes a capital budget as a formal device.
3. Defensible body of analysis which provides criteria to be used as a yardstick for judging uses of funds.
4. Criteria for selection of optimal financing mix.[3]

While the foregoing approach appeals to a sense of logic and embodies a theoretical framework which is scientific and rigorous, a justification of this definition of the finance function as an appropriate normative approach has not been established. Indeed, it becomes difficult under this definition of the finance function to separate it from profit planning or profitability analysis. Professor Solomon makes the following distinction. Finance, he suggests, represents

> the point of contact between the uses of funds within an enterprise and its sources of funds. Profit planning is and should be concerned with all decisions affecting profitability whether or not they require a net increase or decrease in the usage of funds. Financial management as we have defined it is directly involved only when the stock of assets and hence the use of funds is increased or decreased.[4]

This distinction is valid. On the other hand, the domain of profit planning which includes all decisions affecting profitability, whether or not fund-usage is involved, most generally is comprised of financial decisions. In other words, financial decisions, while a subset of profit planning, is a very large subset.

Both the definition of finance as analysis of the *movement* of funds and the broader definition in which the effective *utilization* of funds is emphasized are defensible definitions of the finance function. Each has a strong appeal on intuitive grounds.

Other equally plausible definitions of the finance function have, however, been formulated. At one extreme, it has been said that whenever a decision involves a dollar sign, the finance function is involved. Related to this view is the position that financing is the critical area of the firm. If sufficient funds are available, effective research, production, and marketing policies can be developed. But at the other extreme, the position has also been stated that if the firm has a successful product and sales are growing, adequate financing is assured by the operation of the money and capital markets.

Two things need to be separated. (1) Some functions are solely finance functions. (2) Other functions are mixed, but have a financial content.

To restrict the definition of finance functions to the first class of activities is too restrictive. The second definition includes problems that involve other functional areas. At one extreme, it may be said,

---

[3] *Ibid.*, p. 8.
[4] *Ibid.*, p. 11.

finance always employs accounting information. Hence, in the narrowest view, no decision is purely financial. At the other extreme, few actions do not involve fund flows; hence they have some financial content.

In view of the wide differences in views based on normative definitions of the finance function, this analysis will begin with a descriptive approach to the nature of the finance function. With the background of a factual review of the activities and responsibilities of financial managers, a basis will be provided for stating a set of assumptions that can be developed into a set of propositions about the nature and scope of the finance function.

Functions of Financial Managers

Fortunately, some relatively comprehensive surveys have been made of the activities of financial managers. The studies were conducted by the National Industrial Conference Board and by the American Management Association.[5] Both organizations employed a mail questionnaire approach. Respondents may describe what they do in terms of what sounds attractive or what they would like to regard themselves as doing rather than to describe what they are actually doing. But it is doubtful whether the surveys of financial activities are seriously marred by such imperfections. The questions are relatively straightforward and are seeking only an elementary kind of factual information. Since aspirations and motivations are not involved, the likelihood of significant distortions in responses is relatively small.

Survey Information

As a starting point, therefore, the survey information has useful informational content. The American Management Association survey can be summarized briefly in terms of duties assigned to functionaries more than 50 per cent of the time. Initially, two fundamental types of financial functions are identified: the treasurer function and the controller function.

---

5 See, for example: National Industrial Conference Board, *Duties of Financial Executives* ("Studies in Business Policy," No. 56 [New York: National Industrial Conference Board, 1952]); Norman E. Pflomm, *Managing Company Cash* ("Studies in Business Policy," No. 99 [N.Y.: National Industrial Conference Board, 1961]); Carl G. Baumes, *Division Financial Executives* ("Studies in Business Policy," No. 101 [New York: National Industrial Conference Board, 1961]); Edwin T. Curtis, *Company Organization of the Finance Function* ("American Management Assn. Research Studies," No. 55 [New York: American Management Assn., Inc., 1962]); Elizabeth Marting and Robert E. Finley (eds.), *The Financial Manager's Job* (New York: American Management Assn., 1964).

Using only the first two numerical columns of the table, let us list the duties which are assigned to the treasurer more than 50 per cent of the time. On this basis the treasurer usually has charge of banking relations, cash management, credits and collections, disbursement of dividends, and insurance, all of which represent money or actual possession of funds of some kind.

On the same basis the controller, in his capacity as inspector of financial affairs, usually has control of corporate, general, and cost accounting (90 per cent of the 165 cases); internal auditing (78 per cent); budgeting; preparation of financial statements; centralized office services; preparation of the firm's general payroll; custody, retention, and destruction of records; and systems and procedures.[6]

A clear division of responsibilities appears to emerge. The treasurer is responsible for the acquisition and custody of funds. The main scope of the controller's function is accounting, reporting and control.

Treasury Functions

The foregoing provides a basis for distinguishing the central core in the responsibilities of the treasurer and the controller. With these as central themes, related activities may be indicated.[7] The treasurer typically has responsibility for the acquisition of cash, and therefore, of banking relationships. Contacts with investment bankers would also be in the province of the treasurer. Custodial aspects of the handling of cash would also be the responsibility of the treasurer. As treasurer, he is likely to provide reports on the daily cash position of the firm, the working capital position, and to be responsible for the formulation of cash budgets. In this sense, there is some overlap with the reporting responsibilities of the controller. The point of distinction is that the treasurer is responsible for reports that focus on cash flows and cash conservation.

The survey indicates that the credits and collection activity is generally directly responsible to the treasurer. This is because credit and collection decisions involve the use of funds. But credit and collection policies also have a great impact on the marketing and sales activity of the firm, and, therefore, on the level of production. Thus, the credit activity has an important influence on the sphere of the responsibilities of the sales executives. In a high percentage of cases, the credit and collection activity is responsible to the treasurer's office.

---

[6] Edward T. Curtis, "Company Organization of the Finance Function," *The Financial Manager's Job* (New York City: American Management Assn., Inc., 1957), p. 12.

[7] I wish to reemphasize that this is a descriptive definition of the functions. At this point I am simply summarizing what studies of the responsibilities and activities of financial officers report.

Controller Functions

The controller's central functions are concerned with recording and reporting activities. This implies that the cost and financial accounting operations of the firm are under the supervision and responsibility of the controller. The controller's activity then is a recording of financial information. Various types of reporting responsibilities are related to the accounting activity. Recording and reporting develop into budgeting on the basis of information provided by the operating activities. A natural development, therefore, is a control responsibility.

The analytical and control activities of the controller are related to the internal auditing functions. In 78 per cent of the replies, internal auditing was under the controller's responsibility. On logical grounds, this practice may be questioned. If the controller is responsible for record keeping, there ought to be a separate area responsible for inspecting and reviewing the record keeping and reporting activities of the controller. Related to the control function is custody of records. Record keeping and reporting systems and procedure formulation have, in more than 50 per cent of the cases, been under the responsibility of the controller.

In my own survey of the finance function conducted in 1954, I found that many titles had been employed.[8] This was also the case in the more recent surveys conducted by the American Management Association and the National Industrial Conference Board. Regardless of the titles that are employed, fundamentally there are two basic types of financial officer responsibilities which emerged in these descriptive surveys of financial activities. One is the fund custody responsibility; the other is the record keeping, reporting, and control activities. However, in firms of different sizes, these two major areas of responsibility may be divided in different ways. At the one extreme, in the small firm, the company president typically carries on the fund custody and the main analytical review of reports. At the other extreme, in the larger organization a number of other institutional offices may be created in addition to the offices of the treasury and of the controller.

Vice-President, Finance

In the larger organizations, one of the additional financial officers is the vice-president of finance. Where the vice-president of finance exists, the treasurer generally reports to him. On the other hand, the controller does not necessarily report to the vice-president of finance,

---

8 J. Fred Weston, "The Finance Function," *Journal of Finance*, IX (September, 1954), 265-82.

although he does in a high percentage of cases. Usually, the vice-president of finance supervises and coordinates the work of both the treasurer and controller. Characteristically, he acts as the representative of the financial department to the president and the chairman of the board and formulates general financial policy. When the office exists, the vice-president of finance is also responsible for the analytical aspects of the work of the treasurer and controller.

In the larger firms a fourth corporate officer, whose activities are sometimes considered to be financial in nature, may also be found. This is the corporate secretary. The duties of the corporate secretary focus on written communications relating to the company's financial instruments.

> Finance is perhaps the only corporate function for which there are as many as three members of the top management group in a large corporation. These are the treasurer, the controller, and the vice president of finance. When one remembers that the same large corporation may also have a financial committee of the board of directors with a chairman and the company president, the board chairman, and the board as a whole goes to financial affairs, one realizes that finance is a very important responsibility of top management. In addition, the corporate secretary is sometimes considered to be a financial manager—his duties include issuing and managing documents relating to the corporation as a legal entity and thus take in many aspects of issuing the firm's stocks and bonds.[9]

Thus, the written communications of the corporate secretary encompass legal affairs and recording in connection with top-level committee meetings. His duties include record-keeping in connection with the instruments of ownership and of creditors' claims on the company.

Committees

Finance committees are utilized primarily by the larger enterprises. The rationale for a finance committee stems from the general reasons for the use of committees. These reasons may be briefly summarized. Ideally, a committee assembles different backgrounds and abilities to work on the solution of a problem. For problems of great complexity or which involve a number of management functions and competences, one individual does not possess the number and range of different capabilities required.

The use of a policy committee in a firm illustrates the principle of the use of committees. The policy committee typically includes senior officers from research, engineering, production, marketing, finance, as well as the president of the company. The evaluation of

---

[9] Curtis, *op. cit.*, p. 9.

new product developments, the selection of new markets, salary administration, and other broad policy areas of the firm require the knowledge of functional specialists as well as an overall company point of view. The use of a policy committee brings together the different backgrounds and competences required for the analysis of major policy decision areas.

Finance committees are utilized for two broad types of reasons. The first is that in the acquisition of funds, significant aspects of major money and capital market developments must be clearly understood. These involve developments of broad significance and require a breadth of understanding and careful interpretation. The fund acquisition decisions of a large corporation represent major amounts of funds. A difference of a quarter or a half per cent in the cost of funds represents a large amount of money in absolute terms. Therefore, the judgments and understanding of the senior managers in the organization possessing financial backgrounds are significant. In addition, they may have important contacts and relationships with capital market institutions.

Second, the work of the finance committee involves a resource allocation responsibility. The finance committee will characteristically be responsible for administering the capital and operating budgets. In these resource allocations, some departments and products must necessarily be disappointed. When one segment of the organization is to be limited in relationship to another, some benefits are gained if the decision be a group decision. In this way dissatisfactions and frustrations cannot be centered on any one person. An offsetting risk, however, is that the committee decision may be slow and may represent a degree of compromise which weakens prompt and clear-cut decisions.

Finance committees are sometimes broken into subgroups in the large enterprise. In addition to the general finance committee, there may be a capital appropriations committee which is responsible primarily for capital budgets and expenditures. A budget committee deals primarily with operating budgets. Thus, the capital budgets committee deals with the time horizon of three, five, ten, to twenty years while the operating budgets are concerned with a one-year time horizon. Another subgroup of the general finance committee may be found in a pension committee or a profit-sharing committee. These subcategories of finance committees exist for parallel reasons. The net gains to the enterprise are being allocated. There may exist strong feelings as to the direction in which these gains should go. It is useful to have a committee represent different points of view and to make a group decision. Finally, another subcommittee of the finance committee may be a salary committee. This committee plans the salary administration objectives, sets rates and classifications for top level officers. Again, the reason for having a high level group decision on this point will follow from the previous discussion.

Organization Framework [10]

Thus far, we have provided a descriptive statement of the functions carried on by financial officers. To see the nature of these activities in their full dimensions, it is necessary to look at the finance function in relationship to the general management functions of a firm and the general organization framework. A distinction must be made between generic management functions and specific management functions.

Generic management functions are those which can be performed independent of a specific grouping of activities. A collection of generic management functions is again inherently arbitrary, although it could be argued that a basis for a normative theory could be developed. This would have to be based on empirical evidence that the identification and exercise of a selected group of general management functions resulted in superior performance of firms compared to other firms in which these generic management functions were not recognized. Four to five generic management functions have been identified and are summarized in Table 4-1.

The five areas outlined in Table 4-1 are (1) planning, (2) organizing, (3) directing, (4) controlling, and (5) coordinating. *Planning* is choosing between alternatives. *Organizing* is a division of responsibilities and authority. It also involves a grouping of activities. *Directing* is the exercise of authority. *Controlling* is evaluation of the results of performance. It involves standards, information gathering, analyzing results, and taking necessary corrective action. *Coordinating* is obtaining balance in the operating of the organization structure. Some writers identify this as a fifth function. Other writers argue that if the other generic management functions are carried out effectively, coordination is automatically achieved.

Specific management functions are recognized as production, marketing, finance, and personnel. Production and marketing deal with equipment and products. Personnel deals with human resource management. Production creates time and forms utilities. Marketing is concerned with place utility. In addition to these basic specific management functions which are generally recognized, some writers add specific functions, such as research, engineering, transportation, insurance, real estate, and law. Again, the listing and identification of specific management functions are arbitrary.

Any manager, including functional managers, may be performing

---

10 In the development of the materials in the remainder of this chapter, I have benefited greatly from Harold Koontz and Cyril O'Donnell, *Principles of Management* (New York: McGraw-Hill Book Company, 1964) and from their *Management: A Book of Readings* (New York: McGraw-Hill Book Company, 1964).

Table 4-1: The Major Functions of Management

I. Planning

1. Trends	6. Work assignments
2. Objectives	7. Schedules
3. Policies	8. Growth and expansion
4. Programs	9. Controls and reports
5. Budgets	10. Improvements

II. Organization and Staffing

1. Organization charts	6. Qualification requirements
2. Functional charts	7. Compensation program
3. Position descriptions	8. Staffing and recruitment
4. Performance standards	9. Relationships
5. Job evaluations	10. Personnel utilization

III. Direction and Leadership

1. Delegation	6. Discipline
2. Interpretation	7. Group dynamics
3. Understanding	8. Morale
4. Acceptance of accountability	9. Productivity
5. Training and motivation	10. Job satisfaction

IV. Coordination

1. Communication up, down, across	6. Between H.Q. and Field
2. Integration of all activities	7. With regulatory agencies
3. Within the organization	8. With the industry
4. Within departments	9. With the community
5. Between departments	10. All other relationships

V. Controls: Ratios, Standards

1. Criteria for measuring results	6. Performance appraisals
2. Projects desired results	7. Remedial action
3. Establish check points	8. Work simplification
4. Schedules and time tables	9. Audits and reports
5. Sequence of importance	10. Board approvals

Source: Dick Carlson, *Modern Management* (Paris, France: Organization for Economic Cooperation and Development, 1962), pp. 21-22.

general management activities at any level. In his activity as a financial officer, a controller may have a substantial staff for which he plans, directs, controls, and perhaps coordinates. The financial manager may also be said to be operating a production plant in a sense.

> . . . On the other side, the financial executive is a manager because he heads a working organization which has recently been described as "a plant within a plant." This description stems from the fact that we depend less and less on the clerk, or a multitude of persons, and more and more on elaborate machinery for data recording, summaries and comparison. The financial executive as a manager of this activity in his company is responsible for production—the production of data. We have to be increasingly aware of his dual role whenever we talk about the role of the financial executive in planning. We must distin-

guish between the planning he does in coordination, support and consultation with the other top officers of the company, and the planning he has to do in concert with his staff. He has to prepare his staff for the constant changes in data-processing methods.[11]

Thus, the financial manager is carrying on general management functions in addition to some specific management functions other than the finance function.

Specific functions represent one of the criteria for grouping activities. Activities may be grouped according to products as in firms that might be divided into divisions handling missiles, manned aircraft, space units, etc. Or activities may be grouped on the basis of specific functions such as marketing, research, etc. In addition, activities may be grouped on a geographic basis such as East Coast, Midwest, West Coast, etc. The fundamental basis for grouping is to increase the efficiency with which the activities may be performed.

Finance Function in the Organization Structure

A significant aspect of the place of the finance function in the structure of the organization is that it is centralized. Whatever his title, the financial manager is usually close to the top in the organization structure of the firm. Typically, he is a member of the corporate staff group in a large organization.

The reasons for the centralization of the finance function are twofold. The first reason is that there are economies of scale in carrying out the finance activity. A large issue of securities can be floated on more favorable terms than a smaller one. Large elements of fixed costs are involved in a security flotation. Examples are costs of analysis, legal, accounting, and contact with the Securities and Exchange Commission. Meeting all legal formalities involves some heavy fixed expense. If the total dollar amount of the flotation is large, these are spread over a larger number of dollars, and the costs per dollar of funds raised is smaller. Also, on a large flotation, the firm is likely to have a wider range of fund sources with which to deal.

The second reason the finance function is centralized is that major financial decisions are crucial for the survival of the firm. Decisions which have major financial implications are all major episodes in the life of a corporation. These decisions include: adding a new product line or abandoning an old one, adding a plant or changing location, floating a security issue or entering into leasing arrangements. These decisions have a lasting effect upon the earnings of the firm and, therefore, will require top management consideration.

Of equal importance in conducting the operations of the firm is

---

[11] George Moller, "The Financial Executive In Over-All Company Planning," *The Controller,* XXX (January, 1962), 17.

the need to coordinate the operations of departments or divisions and the performance of the firm as a whole. The operations of individual divisions may be optimal but may use too much of a firm's funds. Thus, the finance function may be centralized in order to achieve over-all optimization.

The Organization Structure of the Firm

For a full understanding of the place of finance in the organization structure, a discussion of the basic authority framework in a large corporation will be useful. The general nature of the relationships is described in Figure 4-1. Beginning at the top is the board of directors which is composed of key management officers and members from outside management. By having members of management on the board of directors, knowledge and understanding about the internal operations of the firm are obtained. The outside board members bring the stockholders' point of view to bear on policies by some board members. Other board members may represent the general public interest.

The president is the chief administrative officer. Below him may be an executive vice-president to whom the group vice-presidents report. It is the relationship between the next two levels in the organization chart that is particularly significant for modern management theory. The functional vice-presidents operate as a corporate level staff group. The functional vice-presidents consist of vice-presidents of engineering, production, finance, marketing, legal, etc. In the next level of the organization are the operations vice-presidents responsible for products, geographic areas, divisions or departments. The organizations under the operations vice-presidents may in turn be organized on a functional, product, or geographic basis. The group vice-presidents have line authority with respect to all activities carried on under their responsibility.

The functional vice-presidents perform as staff advisers to the president. They are basically his staff group. In addition, they act as staff for the operating divisions. They have functional authority to the line departments. Thus, the vice-presidents of marketing will be available for staff discussions, direction, and planning for the line marketing people in each of the line group activities. However, line authority under the marketing people in the group activity is exercised by the operations vice-president. Similarly, the vice-president of finance or other corporate staff financial officers, report directly to the president in a staff capacity. In addition, they may exercise guidance over financial officers attached to the operating divisions or group activities.

The nature of the responsibility of divisional or operations financial executives is derived from the logic of these organization relationships.

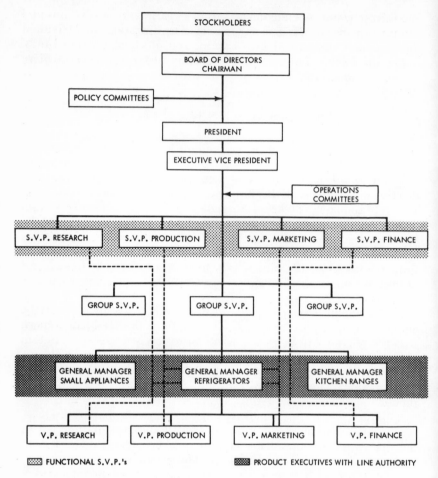

Figure 4-1. Corporate Organization Structure

With respect to the custody of funds responsibility, the operating financial executives have relatively little activity to perform. The fund-raising activities are performed at a relatively high level in the organization. The treasurer's activity is centralized at the corporate level. The recording, reporting, and analysis activities are carried on under the controller. The controller prescribes forms and procedures for all of the operating activities. This provides a basis for coordinating reports and analysis. It also facilitates rapid comparisons of plans with actual performance. Any special needs of reports, analysis, or controls that the operating executives may have in the divisions will also be carried out by the divisional financial executive. However, the special reports and requirements placed on the divisional financial executives by the operating divisional financial executives must be consistent with the divisional financial executive's responsibilities to the corporate vice-president, in this instance the controller.

The divided responsibilities of operating financial executives gives rise to a dilemma with regard to the evaluation of performance. If the supervision and evaluation of divisional financial executives are performed at the corporate vice-presidential level, the divisional financial executives may not work responsively with the line officers in the division. On the other hand, if they are evaluated by the line officers in the divisions, they may not cooperate in providing the corporate level financial officers with requisite reports and controls.

The corporate level financial officers should receive evaluation reports on the performance of divisional vice-presidents from the divisional operating line executives. The final evaluation and recommendations as to salary levels, promotions, etc., however, should be performed by the treasurer or controller. In this manner, cooperation with operating executives is stimulated by their evaluation authority. Since the final decisions are made by the corporate level financial officers, the essential coordination of financial activities throughout the enterprise will, thereby, be facilitated.

This problem of a relationship between the corporate level vice-presidents and line executives in relationship to the divisional finance people has been effectively described by Professor Simon.

> One of the questions we explored was whether it was better to have a "dotted line" or a "solid line" of authority from the factory controller or regional sales accounting executive to the company controller. In most of the companies we studied, the formal authority arrangements did not appear to make much difference. Whatever the formal arrangement, the factory controller, for example, generally looked to the home office controller's department for instructions on the technical aspects of his job, and to the factory manager for special assignments and activities to improve controllership service to the factory.[12]

The logic of the distinctions set out by Professor Simon is persuasive. Uniformity in accounting reports requires that the divisional financial people be responsible to the corporate controller for the technical aspects of their assignments. With reference to operating activities, their responsibility is to the line executives in the divisions.

The framework provided in Figure 4-1 also indicates the role of committees. Policy committees are shown intervening between the board of directors and the president. They are responsible for establishing the broad, over-all guidelines for corporate activities. Policy committees are smaller in number than the board of directors but achieve representation from two levels: (1) board of directors, and (2) the

---

12 Herbert A. Simon, "Organizing for Controllership: Centralizing and Decentralization," *Controller*, January, 1955, 13.

functional vice-presidents. Thus, policy formulation will reflect the viewpoint of the top governing board in the corporation and the viewpoint of the functional specialists who are not responsible for operations. Therefore, the points of view represented in the policy committees are both broad and yet responsible.

Intervening between the president and the functional vice-presidents are the operations committees. The operations committees are charged with the responsibility for coordinating the allocation of activities and resources at the operations level of the firm within the policy framework laid down by the policy committee. Since the emphasis is on operations, representation from the line vice-presidents is heavy. On the other hand, since the requirement is for coordination of operations in the different divisions or groups, representation of the functional vice-presidents is also required.

The policy committees are composed mainly of representatives from the board of directors and the functional vice-presidents. They are responsible for the general policy of the corporation. As Alfred P. Sloan, Jr. argued, "this committee should be a policy group detached from the interests of specific operating divisions. In other words, it should contain only general executives." [13] The operations committee, however, is composed of representatives of both the functional vice-presidents and the line executives. Thus, for coordination purposes, the operating divisions had the opportunity to have their point of view expressed. However, Mr. Sloan emphasized that the operations committees were not policy-making bodies, "but only a forum for policy." [14] Participation in such discussions develops understanding and acceptance of the policies formulated.

The type of organization described above may now be regarded as characteristic of the large American corporation. It was developed to meet the kinds of problems involved in the multi-product, multi-plant firms that emerged in the United States at the turn of the century. Mr. Sloan described the problem that was faced by the General Motors Corporation in the early 1920's.

> It was a case of competition among the divisions for available capital and all of different preferences among the leading officers. A number of specific instances brought home to me, and to others, the fact that we lacked a proper procedure for handling appropriations. In the Executive Committee the practical workings were that each member with divisional responsibility needed the support of other members for his own capital requests. This horse trading meant that, as I wrote in a later study of our procedure, from the practical standpoint . . . the supervision supposed to be exercised by the Executive Committee

---

13 Alfred P. Sloan, Jr., "My Years with General Motors—Part III," *Fortune*, November, 1963, p. 169.

14 *Ibid.*, p. 169.

was more theoretical than practical. With a shortage of funds to meet all demands, principal attention thereupon was given not to the question of how to divide scarce investment funds but how to raise more money.[15]

The problems faced were essentially lack of a rational basis for allocating corporate resources among the individual operating units. Basically, it was a problem in lack of effective financial planning and control. What are the remedies?

The remedies essentially involved curtailing the excessive freedom of the divisions, which had gone so far as to jeopardize the survival of the corporation. The corporation could not afford to let its divisions continue to make the kind of mistakes they were making: the weak divisions threatened the existence of the strong ones, and the strong ones themselves were operated more for their own than the corporation's interest. The necessary centralizing remedies—largely operating controls—created a temporary distortion in our general policy which later had to be corrected in order to return to a workable decentralization. These are the areas where we took action: appropriations, for capital spending; cash control; inventory control; production control.[16]

What followed was essentially the broad outlines of an organization with both centralized and decentralized characteristics. The basic solution was centralized policy and control with decentralized operations.

In addition to this *organization* framework, the *processes* of effective planning and control were required. Mr. Sloan expressed it briefly as follows:

Two things were involved in correcting the situation: first, the art of forecasting, and second, the problem of shortening the reaction time when a forecast proved wrong—and a forecast, I might add, can be wrong even in this day of complex mathematical forecasting techniques.[17]

How effective planning and control are achieved varies with the individual organization and the nature of the business, but these are among the central processes involved in the effective operations of a business firm. An analysis of the functions of planning and control will also help illustrate more fully the nature of the essential functions performed by financial executives. This is the task of the following chapter.

---

[15] *Op. cit.*, p. 169.
[16] *Ibid.*, p. 169.
[17] *Ibid.*, p. 203.

```
5555555555555555555555555555555555555555555555555555555555555555555555555555555555555
5555555555555555555555555555555555555555555555555555555555555555555555555555555555555
55555555555555555555555555555555555555    5555555555    5555555555555555555555555555555555555
5555555555555555555555555555555555555    5555555555    5555555555555555555555555555555555555
55555555555555555555555555555555555    555555555    5555555555555555555555555555555555555
5555555555555555555555555555555555    5555555    5555555555555555555555555555555555555
555555555555555555555555555555555    55555    5555555555555555555555555555555555555
55555555555555555555555555555555    555    5555555555555555555555555555555555555
5555555555555555555555555555555    5    5555555555555555555555555555555555555
5555555555555555555555555555555    5555555555555555555555555555555555555
55555555555555555555555555555    5555555555555555555555555555555555555
55555555555555555555555555    5555555555555555555555555555555555555
555555555555555555555555555555555555555555555555555555555555555555555555555555555555
5555555555555555555555555555555555555555555555555555555555555555555555555555555555555
```

The Finance Function and
Financial Policy

ONE VIEW of the finance function that has been emphasized in finance textbooks is the analysis of the flow of funds,[1] and all writers agree that this is an important aspect of the field. Other writers recognize that financial planning and control are important endeavors and also mention a wide variety of activities, such as mergers and compensation arrangements. These numerous aspects of finances, however, may be placed in a systematic framework, and it is the objective of this chapter to do so.

Overview of Financial Decision Areas

Three central decision areas of finance may be identified as: (1) leverage or financing mix, (2) liquidity, and (3) the utilization of the net income of the firm. Decisions concerning leverage or financing mix may properly be regarded as the central problem of finance. Regardless of the theoretical arguments about a firm increasing its value by

---

[1] Cf. Harry G. Guthmann and Herbert E. Dougall, *Corporate Financial Policy* (Englewood Cliffs, N.J.: Prentice-Hall, Inc., 1940), p. 1; Pearson Hunt, Charles Williams, and Gordon Donaldson, *Basic Business Finance* (Homewood, Ill.: Richard D. Irwin, Inc., 1958), pp. 3-4; Robert W. Johnson, *Financial Management* (Boston: Allyn and Bacon, Inc., 1962), pp. 12-14.

changing its financing mix, differences in degree of leverage are observed and are found to exist among firms in the same industry and among different industries. One of the facts of business life that the student of finance seeks to explain is the observed differences in the degree of financial leverage employed.

The second area of financial decision-making, liquidity, may be seen as a constraint on risk assumption or as an aspect of risk-limiting behavior by business firms. Differences in liquidity are also found and exist among firms in the same industry and among different industries.

The third area of financial analysis is the utilization of net income. To what extent should net income be allocated to the owners of firms? To what extent should the rate of growth of the firm be dependent upon the availability of net income?

The latter set of questions relates to decisions about the rate and direction of growth of the firm. Such considerations make necessary a study of the planning and control activities of the firm. In turn, planning and control activities are related to decisions regarding resource allocation in the firm among different products and among different departments. Consideration of resource allocation and utilization suggests that finance may be concerned with *analysis* of decisions of all types since they involve the use of funds and the utilization of resources. Analysis relates to the determination of capital values and their changes. Thus, a consideration of the central decision areas faced by the firm results in a considerable proliferation of the types of activities related to the finance function. A brief review of some of the major decision areas of the firm will indicate those types of activities for which financial managers have a major responsibility and those types of activities for which financial managers have at least partial responsibility.

Leverage Decisions

At the most general level, leverage decisions involve at least three types: (1) operating leverage, (2) financial leverage, and (3) time leverage.

Operating leverage   The characteristics of operating leverage can be illustrated by reference to break-even analysis. Break-even analysis presents the terms of the trade-off between fixed commitments and flexibility.[2] If the firm has a considerable investment in plant and

---

2 Break-even analysis suffers from its inadequate attention to the elasticity of demand and, therefore, is not useful for pricing and output decisions. Break-even analysis, however, is valuable for consideration of operating leverage if demand characteristics are given. The implications of decisions on flexibility and adaptability in the choice of a fixed plant were set out analytically by George Stigler, "Production and Distribution in the Short Run," *Journal of Political Economy,* XLVII (June, 1939), 305-27.

equipment, as volume increases, the additional labor required to complete the item should be small. When a firm has low fixed costs, we would expect variable costs to be higher. If Firm A has fixed costs of $10 million, its variable costs might be .6 of sales. If Firm B has fixed costs of $1 million, we would expect to observe a higher variable cost. Its total cost function might be: total cost is equal to $1 million plus .9 of sales. As a consequence of this difference in the cost structure of the two firms, Firm A on a small volume may lose money. But for any increase in volume after the break-even point is passed, the elasticity of profit increase for Firm A is much higher than for Firm B after Firm B crosses its break-even point.

The decisions as to which of these two structures is better involves analysis related to the expected volume of operations of the two firms and the degree of expected variability in the volume of operations in these two firms. This is a critical area for the chief decision and policy makers in a firm. The extent to which the firm is willing to expose itself to the risk of loss on fixed outlays is related to the expected volume of operations on the outlays for this particular product line. The risks are in both directions. Some risks are reduced by economizing on fixed outlays. The firm with larger fixed outlays may, however, for a given volume of operations be able to produce at a much lower cost per unit. If Firm A is able to operate at a much lower cost per unit, Firm B's policy of seeking to minimize risk by minimizing fixed outlays may cause its costs and prices to be higher for large volumes. A firm cannot avoid some types of risks. The effective business planner accepts exposure to the kinds of risks that are appropriate for the environment in which the firm is operating. This is effective risk management in a broad sense.

Financial leverage   Operating leverage relates to choice of the asset mix—both the total amount of assets and the asset mix. In a similar fashion, one can consider financing leverage in analyzing the right-hand side of the balance sheet. Just as asset management can be analyzed in terms of break-even analysis for operating costs, one can analyze financial decision-making in terms of break-even analysis for financial leverage. In this context financing leverage refers not only to the use of debt versus equity funds but also to the terms of the financing mix.

There is another aspect of leverage that is logically encompassed by the categories of operating leverage and financing leverage but is somehow missed when talking about the devices for analyzing, operating, and financing leverage. The third aspect is "time leverage."

Time leverage   Let us examine the revenue prospects for a firm over time. In Figure 5-1, time is on the horizontal axis. The vertical axis depicts the level of net revenue. With its existing product family, a firm sees its volume of revenues grow at 5 per cent per annum for about three years, and beyond three years visibility begins to dim. This is the revenue outlook for the firm if it does not add to its product family and would be clearly true for a firm in the defense market or in industrial machinery. This might not be true for a soap manufacturer, because people will continue to buy his product. However, people may not continue to buy those particular products that the firm is manufacturing. If his revenue volume is to continue, he will need to produce a different product family. Recognizing the problem, the firm has a number of strategic choices. It can make small outlays to achieve modest net additions to revenue. Or, it can incur large outlays for an extended period of time with the possibility of achieving a new breakthrough, such as computers or semiconductors, or nuclear inspection devices. It may seek to sell products that will have tremendous markets so that the firm will be in a unique and protected position for a substantial period of time. A firm does not ordinarily achieve such situations with small outlays. A major strategic decision is to determine the extent to which the firm makes the low-risk, low-return kind of investment versus the high-risk, high-potential possibility kind of investment.

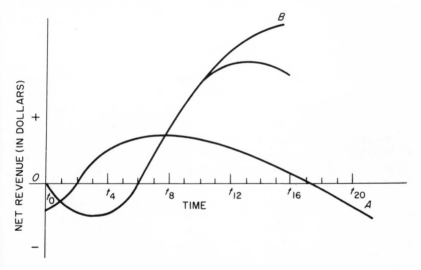

Figure 5-1. Illustration of Time Leverage

In its long-range planning strategy, a firm may have a time-phasing of a family of these types of investments. In analyzing and formulating such strategic decisions, the financial manager plays an important role. He has an important function to perform in guiding the firm to make solid determinations in areas that affect the long-run viability of the firm.

Related to the three concepts of leverage is the relationship between the total amount of assets a firm owns and its sales. A number
of policies offers the opportunity for minimizing the investment in
fixed assets. Some may decrease fixed costs, others may increase them.
For example, a fixed lease agreement will require fixed rental outlays
over a period of time. Or, alternatively, a lease agreement may make
the payment a specified percentage of the firm's gross income; or
investment in fixed assets may be reduced by utilizing used equipment rather than new equipment. The degree of vertical integration
will influence the amount of a firm's investment in assets in relationship to sales. To the extent that a firm is manufacturing all the parts
of a final assembly unit, it will have a larger investment in machinery
and work in process inventories. If a firm is merely assembling an
item, the length of the production cycle is likely to be reduced, and
the amount of work-in-process inventories would be substantially
lower.

For financing the assets, other kinds of choices must be made. A
basic choice is the decision of the ratio of financing by owners' money
versus creditors'. Wide variations are observed in practice. Contrasts
can be drawn between a firm such as DuPont which raises virtually
none of its financing from debt and a small, new, growing firm in the
advanced technology industries which may be using leverage to the
extent of $6 to $7 of creditors' money to $1 of owners' money. In
addition to decisions between owners' and creditors' money, other
strategic financing choices must be made. If debt is emphasized, choices
between short-term and long-term financing must be made. Different
forms of debt involve different credit standards and different terms
of financing. In addition, options to convert debt into varying forms
of equity claims may be granted. The number of possible arrangements of these variables is literally infinite.

We have thus seen how operating and financial leverage decisions
are intertwined. Leverage decisions are also related to liquidity decisions since the amount of investment in receivables will influence certain types of liquidity measures. In addition, the extent to which
funds are raised from short-term sources versus long-term sources will
affect the current ratio and its variants. Leverage decisions and the
utilization of net income are also interdependent and, in turn, related
to the firm's goals with regard to its growth rate of sales and earnings.
The disposition of the firm's net income will determine the extent to
which funds are available from internal sources. On the other hand,
the firm's decisions about its goals for rate of growth influence the
amount of funds that will be required. The combination of the
amount of funds required and the amount available from internal
sources will determine the amount of funds required from external
sources. At this point decisions about external funds from debt versus
equity sources will be required.

The foregoing discussion of the relationship between leverage, liquidity, and the utilization of net income have demonstrated the close interrelationships between decisions in each of these three major areas. These decisions are related to a wide variety of other research, production, and operating decisions of the business firm. To bring all of these aspects of the operation of the firm into focus is one of the important functions of financial planning and control.

Financial Planning and Control

Planning and control have become the central contribution and responsibility of the finance function. As one writer expressed it:

Total financial planning, as the phrase is used here, embraces the advance programming of all the plans of financial management and the integration and coordination of these plans with the operating plans of the other functions of the enterprise. As a process, therefore, total financial planning comprises the following steps:

1. Estimating the resources that will be required to execute the operating plans of the business.
2. Determining how much of these resources can be generated by the business itself and how much will have to be obtained elsewhere.
3. Identifying the best means and sources for obtaining additional resources when they are required.
4. Establishing the best method of applying *all* resources (self-generated and acquired) to execute the operating plans.[3]

Planning and control activities have been associated with a "revolution" in management methods.

What is this new way of managing which constitutes the core of the management revolution of our time?

First, it consists of organizing so as to push the profit motive as far down the organization as possible.

Second, it consists of adopting the concept of management planning and control.

Third, it consists of building an organization which can help the president carry out his job of coordinating the parts, and which can supply him with the tools of management planning and control.[4]

This new concept of the nature of planning and control has been summarized briefly as follows:

---

3 Robert Jerrett, Jr., "Integrating and Coordinating the Treasury and Controllership Functions," *The Financial Manager's Job* (New York: American Management Assn., Inc., 1957), pp. 37-38.

4 T. F. Bradshaw, "The Status of the Financial Executive Today," *The Financial Executive's Job* ("Financial Management Series," No. 99 [New York: American Management Assn., Inc., 1952]), p. 17.

The new way of management has been summed up in the phrase "management planning and control." By management planning and control, I mean acceptance of the importance and validity of certain objectives. These are the objectives: First, setting a profit goal; second, setting departmental goals which taken together, will achieve the profit goal; third, measuring to keep the whole organization moving in balance toward the goal. The tools of control are not nearly so important as a clear realization of the ends to be attained. Each company which has substituted navigational flying for seat-of-the-pants flying has developed its own kit of tools.[5]

These activities of planning and control are of such central importance that an understanding of the nature of the finance function cannot be achieved without indicating more explicitly what is involved in the process. First, we shall analyze the nature of planning.

We begin with a discussion of the relation of finance to the general functions of planning, organizing, directing, and controlling. It is clear that finance has an important role to play in the planning. We have defined planning as a formulation of alternatives and the development of criteria for selecting or choosing between the alternatives. This is the concept of planning in general terms. The specific mechanics of planning involve a number of steps.

Step one is planning to plan. By this is really meant planning as a process. Planning is an attitude; it is a way of life. Planning is a process of having people interact in a particular way. The significant thing about the particular way people interact is to attack problems that are ill-structured for which we do not have mechanical procedures for arriving at a most efficient or optimum solution. What is distinctive about this process is closing the loop in an iterative fashion, that is, going around all aspects of the problem in terms of the steps that will be next enumerated.

The next step is defining goals. The goals of a business firm are defined most clearly initially in financial terms. These are: a target return on investment (20 per cent after taxes); a growth rate in earnings per share per annum (8 per cent); some goal of stability in earnings per share over time (no decline exceeding 25 per cent). There may be some subsidiary financial goals in terms of liquidity measures or leverage measures as well as the profitability, stability, and growth. These are not mutually exclusive categories.

A second important dimension in which the goals of a firm are defined is choosing the firm's industry. A firm often limits itself to its traditional product lines but should not because of diversification opportunities. Within an industry, there are many alternative segments in which a firm may operate. To define an industry for the firm means to select a concentric group of products—a group of products that has

---

[5] *Ibid.*, p. 18.

some common thread between them. Defining the industry is an important aspect of stating the firm's goals.

A third aspect of planning is defining the firm's position in the industry with regard to some critical aspects of policy. Are they going to be small margin and high volume producers? Will they emphasize quality? Will they emphasize service? Will the firm use its own sales organization? Or, will the firm use other parts of the distributive mechanism such as manufacturers' agents, jobbers, or others? There is a large number of variables in terms of its position in the industry that the firm seeks to play.

Fourth, goals may be stated in terms of the role the firm seeks to play as a part of organized society. This includes the social responsibilities of the business firm and the relationship of the firm to other power groups in the society. Other power groups are government, labor unions, the public as a whole, foreign competitors, domestic competitors. Essentially, this is a matter of self-identification, as if the firm were an individual.

Step number five is identifying the environment in which the firm has chosen to operate. A firm in many ways is like a mortal animal. It exists in an environment, and the Darwinian process will proceed. The environment will adopt or reject the animal in terms of its characteristics. The firm has a little more flexibility. The firm adapts perhaps more readily to its environment if it has clearly identified what the strategic elements in its environment are.

Step six is identifying what it takes to succeed in that environment. A firm can make a matrix in terms of the characteristics of the environment, what it takes to succeed in the environment. It should then compare a profile of assessing the firm's capabilities in relationship to its environment and what it takes to succeed. The following basic question should be answered: what kind of firm succeeds best in this environment?

We then analyze a profile of this firm, a profile of its competitors, and of other firms in the industry. This analysis will enable the firm to look down the road five, ten, fifteen or twenty years (one of the important functions of long-range planning) to see what characteristics of the environment are going to require for survival in relation to other firms. This plan may suggest possibilities for mergers. For example, the firm may be a weak entity in the industry and might be complemented by some of the other weak entities.

When we reach step seven, we have defined goals, we have identified the environment, we have assessed capabilities—both in absolute and relative terms. Given these factors, we may now identify and assess the several strategies which exist for achieving the firm's goals. It is useful to illustrate the fact that there would be a number of strategies the firm might adopt. Let us suppose one is to employ scientists to emphasize advanced technical capability in the firm. In this case, a firm may stress products, or R & D programs, or a merger acquisition program. Or, it may, moreover, choose to emphasize growth. There is a large range of available strategies from which the firm might select, and it involves sales, policies, people, facilities, or technical capabilities. Assessment of these plans and strategies is accomplished in terms of financial consequences, such as profitability.

Step eight is formulation of derivative operational plans, after a strategy has been adopted. There is no point in going to step eight until a plan has been adopted, because with each long-range plan is associated its own family of derivative operational plans. The derivative operational plans involve an implementation and an integration of long-range plans and short-range plans.

Step nine is an information system which provides for (a) information flow, (b) monitoring of results, and (c) feedback, adjustments and corrections. This provides a basis for comparing goals, objectives, and results. It obviously also involves having standards or controls which provide a basis for comparing results against some norms.

Step ten would involve corrective actions, either to avoid deficiencies or to improve the activities of business operations.

The purpose of setting out ten steps of planning is to illustrate the basic theme that the finance function, while a specific management function, has an important responsibility in carrying out generic management functions. The foregoing has described in detail the planning function and has indicated the numerous ways in which the finance function plays an integral role in this process. Also, the planning process provides a framework for giving directions, so we have also illustrated briefly the function of direction. Since organization involves a grouping of activities to increase efficiency, finance is very clearly a mechanism for setting up information flows that provides a basis for intelligent grouping of activities and assigning authority and responsibility. Control may next be examined more fully.

The Finance Function and the General Control Function

The nature of the control function may now be set out more explicitly. Fundamentally, in the analysis of the enterprise as a system, a flow of at least six fundamental factors is involved: (1) orders, (2) materials or energy, (3) people, (4) capital equipment, (5) information, (6) funds. The central control problem involves keeping track of these flows. The general denominator is through the use of information flows. Fundamentally, a system of control involves obtaining information, recording it, storing it, processing information, information retrieval, information analysis, and the use of information to alter and improve the operations of the firm. As described previously and as emphasized by Mr. Sloan, planning and control are related.[6] Planning is necessary to establish goals and standards. Control is necessary to obtain information promptly, to compare plans and performance, and to provide a vehicle for a feedback process in which the system can be altered to achieve improved performance.

An original and analytical approach to the control problem has been developed by Andrew C. Stedry.[7] His approach is in the spirit of the behavioral theory of the firm. Stedry focuses on the relations between goals, aspirations, and the expected actual level of expenditure as critical variables. He formulates and tests a set of postulates. The following symbols are employed to permit a brief statement of his postulates.[8]

H = the department head
E = expected actual level of expenditure
A = aspired level of expenditure
B = budgeted level of expenditure
D = discouragement point
F = failure point

(1) If E does not equal A, H will move A toward E.
(2) If E does not equal A and B is lowered, H will reduce his A.
(3) If $(E - A) < D$, H will be encouraged and seek to reduce E.
(4) If $F > (E - A) > D$, H will be discouraged.
(5) If $(E - A) > F$, H will resign.

Professor Stedry has raised fundamental questions about the role of budgets, standard costs, and standards. He views these as equivalent to goals. My own experience suggests that budgets are more like an instrument for a sequential improvement in revenue and cost elements than ends or goals. Further, by comparing the difference between projections and actual, increased understanding of the disturbing influences may be achieved. Of great importance in the budgeting process are analytical reviews of the variances and their causes. Increased understanding of the processes of the firm may, thereby, be achieved.

There is danger in over-generalizing on the nature of the budget process. Stedry and others refer to budgets as imposed by higher authorities on department heads.[9] From my own experience, I have

---

[6] While related, planning and control responsibilities in the organization structure should be separated, because different types of capabilities are required and because control should be used as a check on the effectiveness of the planning process.

[7] Andrew C. Stedry, *Budget Control and Cost Behavior* (Englewood Cliffs, N.J.: Prentice-Hall, Inc., 1960).

[8] *Ibid.*, pp. 23-28.

[9] *Ibid.*, pp. 5-12 and references therein cited.

companies in which other techniques are employed such as the ce of having the responsible department head set his own revenue and cost estimates. The control over his setting these too low is that his projected performance can be compared with different departments or with similar activities in the same or in other firms. If he "plays it safe," he will present an inferior performance projection and may have his resource allocations decreased. Furthermore, if the department head makes his own initial estimates of revenues, costs, and resource requirements, he has provided a basis for comparison with the actual performance subsequently achieved. These confrontations of the estimated and the actual provide a good test of the department head's knowledge and understanding of the product market and competitive environment and his own department's cost activity in relation to revenues.

Role of Financial Managers in Planning and Control

The role of finance in the planning and control process is now treated. One point of view emphasizes that in the process of handling information flows, the financial manager obtains the "authority of knowledge." Because of his familiarity with all aspects of the operations of the enterprise, he becomes an important decision maker in the process. Not only is it sometimes argued that the financial executive takes on an important role in operating decisions because of his knowledge of both individual activities and the over-all operations of the firm, it is also said that it is necessary that the finance person should fully familiarize himself with operations.

> As these steps suggest, financial planning cannot be considered a function distinct and separate from the other planning activities of the enterprise in the concept of total financial planning. Just as profit consciousness, must be instilled in all operating employees, so should "operations consciousness" be instilled in the financial planning process. This can be achieved in many ways. Sometimes the financial man will independently familiarize himself with operating problems and thus avoid having to perform his functions "by the numbers," or without regard for the changing nature of operations. Financial people also can be intentionally exposed to operating areas through direct assignment or committee participation to help them gain a greater breadth of understanding of the business and learn what is behind the figures.[10]

This point of view argues that there are two reasons for finance people to be intimately familiar with operations. One is that without this familiarity he will perform his record-keeping functions in a mechanical way. To determine what information is required and

---

[10] Jerrett, *op. cit.*, p. 38.

how it should be organized requires a full understanding of the needs of the operation. Second, it is said that financial people should be sensitive to the needs of operations, just as operating people should be sensitive to the needs of conservation of funds and profit planning.

A directly opposite point of view has been expressed.

> Specifically, analysis should be a function separate from accounting. The distinction between the two is clear enough. Accounting compiles and reports the financial record of the past—the things that have happened and the results that have been obtained. Analysis (as the word is used here) on the other hand, deals with the future. It applies intelligence to data of past operation in order to throw light on the problems of future operation. It deals with actions to be taken and decisions to be made.
>
> As a function, therefore, analysis is coordinate with the other principal financial functions.[11]

This point of view argues that accounting is concerned with compiling reports, whereas analysis is a separate function. In this distinction one might argue that accounting is responsible for record keeping and is historical in its orientation. Finance is responsible for analysis, budgeting, and forecasting.

In his survey of the activities of controllers, Professor Simon also argued for separation between record keeping and report preparation with analysis.

> Thus far we have said nothing about the activities of the controller's department that bulks largest in terms of numbers of personnel and work-load—the record-keeping and report-preparation functions. It was our general observation that these controller's departments operated most effectively, which provided a considerable measure of separation between these functions on the one hand, and the analytic functions on the other. When important responsibilities for analytic duties and important responsibilities for the supervision of record-keeping and report-preparation rests on a single man or a single unit, the former tended to suffer in the time and attention that was given them. The pressure of regular deadlines and the tasks of supervising clerical personnel gave the day-to-day activities priority over equally important, but postponable, analytic tasks. The simplest and perhaps the only practicable way to maintain a balanced allocation of effort appeared to be to vest these responsibilities in separate units.[12]

In my judgment there is no logical or normative basis for arguing that record keeping and report preparation should be kept separate from analysis. The degree to which the financial officer engages in

---

11 Alvin Brown, *Financial Approach to Industrial Operations* (New York: Society for the Advancement of Management, 1957), p. 11.

12 Herbert A. Simon, "Organizing for Controllership: Centralization and Decentralization," *Controller*, January, 1955, p. 13.

analysis and the extent to which he participates in operating decisions depends on the individual. If the financial officer has a broad background by virtue of education or experience that enables him to participate effectively in operating decisions, he most probably will participate. If he is a strong personality, he is particularly the one most likely to enter actively in the strategic decision-making process of the firm.

The financial officer participates in the important operating decisions of the firm because of his close contact with all of the vital intelligence information in the operations of the business firm. Also, in connection with compiling forecasts and performing analysis of the results of operations, he acquires a knowledge and familiarity with the nature of operations. Therefore, the financial manager may actively participate in operating decisions if either his (1) background in education or training, (2) general ability, or (3) personality drive leads him to so participate. Where the combination of all three prerequisites is present, the financial officer may make a substantial contribution to the operating activities of the firm. The great danger, however, is the situation in which the financial officer may possess the third attribute but not the first two. In this case, his contact with vital information flows of the firm may lead him to desire to participate in one form or another in the decision-making process. Lacking the background or ability to participate, however, he may introduce an element of friction and may represent an impediment to effective decision making in the firm.

The Range of Financial Policies

The foregoing review of financial activities reveals a wide diversity of responsibilities. For some activities and some firms, the financial manager may take a major responsibility. In other firms, his responsibility for these activities may be relatively small. To focus the wide variety of activities related to the financial manager, it may be useful to summarize the responsibilities of financial management in terms of the major types of financial policies. It will be remembered that in our discussion of methodology, policies were defined as guides to decision making. The nature of the finance function may be made more meaningful by describing the characteristics and scope of financial policies.

Since policies seek to contribute to the achievement of goals and objectives of the firm, some illustrative objectives must be first specified. A number of possible objectives are the following:

1. Growth in sales of 8 per cent per annum
2. Growth in earnings per share of 10 per cent per annum
3. Growth in market price per share of 12 per cent per annum

4. A price earnings ratio for common stock of over 20
5. A profit margin on sales of 5 to 6 per cent after taxes
6. A return on investment of 14 per cent after taxes

Financial policies seek to contribute to the attainment of such objectives. Three areas that represent financial policies relate to decisions with respect to liquidity, leverage, and the use of earnings. With
respect to liquidity, the firm may adopt a number of policies. Some
illustrative liquidity policies are stated. The current ratio shall not
fall below 2.5 to 1. Marketable securities shall not fall below 2 million dollars. The quick ratio shall be at least 1.5 to 1. Inventories shall
not exceed .5 of net working capital. Expressed in such concise quanti-
tative fashion these relationships appear also to constitute financial
standards. They are policies also in the sense that individual decisions will be guided by them.

With respect to leverage, a financial policy of a firm may be to
have a target debt to equity ratio of 50 per cent. Thus, as the firm ex-
pands, the choice between long-term debt and common stock as a
source of incremental financing may be determined by the decision
rule (i.e., policy) that the debt to equity ratio will not exceed 50 per
cent over a period of time. This would permit the debt to equity ratio
to exceed 50 per cent temporarily in the expectation of an addition
to equity from retained earnings over a specified number of years. Or
conversely, it would permit the sale of common stock which brings
the debt ratio substantially below 50 per cent in the anticipation of
increasing debt at a future date. Another financial policy may be to
have 40 per cent of long term debt in convertibles. A related financial
policy may be to employ subordinated debt to the extent of 20 per
cent of the net worth of the firm. The use of convertible preferred
stocks in mergers and acquisitions may also reflect a basic corporate
financial policy.

With respect to timing, the firm may have the financial policy of
considering an equity flotation to finance future growth whenever
the price earnings ratio on the firm's common stock exceeds 25 or 30
times or some other designated multiplier. An alternative policy may
be to sell debt when the cost of long-term money falls below 4 per
cent per annum for the firm. If the sale of equity results in a decline
of the debt ratio below 50 per cent, new money may be raised subsequently by debt issues. If the sale of debt results in a rise in the
debt ratio above 50 per cent, the firm may plan to return to the target
debt to equity ratio by retained earnings plowback and by equity
issues when the common stock price earnings ratio rises above the
designated level.

A firm may seek to maintain a target dividend payout of 55 per
cent of earnings on the average. Or the firm may seek to achieve a
growth in dividends per share of 7 per cent per annum. A firm may

have a policy of paying no cash dividends but to pay stock dividends equal to the annual growth in the firm's book value per share. A firm may have a policy of employing no external funds and to limit its growth in assets to an amount per year which can be achieved by a retention of 80 per cent of earnings. Or, more generally, a firm may formulate a policy in which the amount of its investment is a specified percentage (over or under 100 per cent) of its earnings available to common stockholders. An alternative use of earnings may specify that the firm follow the policy of acquiring its own stock when the market value of the common stock falls below its book value by some specified percentage. The distribution of the net income of the firm suggest policies with regard to the utilization of the operating income of the firm. These policies may deal with profit sharing, stock options, and relating incentives to performance generally.

Relating growth to earnings is also affected by the extent to which the firm shall own versus lease its operating plant and equipment. Leasing provides for the acquisition and financing of assets. Mergers and acquisitions may accomplish the acquisition of assets, of managements and of organizations as well. A firm may have the policy of expanding horizontally by internal growth and expanding vertically by merger, or a firm could have the policy of actively considering mergers whenever its price earnings ratio rises above 30. Firms in new technologies but related markets may then be acquired.

The foregoing illustrations of financial policies suggest the wide range of responsibilities of financial managers. These responsibilities have great significance for the performance of the individual firm. But, in addition, financial decisions and policies also have important significance for the operation of the economy. Reciprocally, the financial and economic environment have important influence on the timing and nature of financial decisions. To provide a framework for an understanding of these relationships, Chapter 6 provides an interim restatement of and the emerging influences on the nature of the finance function.

Emerging Trends and the Finance Function

Delineation of the Finance Function

THE EXTENDED discussion of the preceding chapters makes possible a succinct summary statement of the nature of the finance function, the relevant aspects of which are outlined in Table 6-1. The table sets out four major aspects of the finance function identified as (1) funds flows, (2) maximizing capital value, (3) information flows, and (4) planning and control.

The activities included in the finance function represent a continuum. The first two categories under Section *A* of the table relate to specific finance functions, while the second two categories under Section *B* relate to generic management functions. Interrelations exist, however, between the activities of the financial manager, because the operation of the business firm represents the behavior of a total system. Increasingly, a total systems approach will be taken to the operation of business firms to encompass finance as well as other business management functions. A major goal of financial management is the acquisition of funds at the lowest cost and under the best terms. It is also concerned with the effective utilization of those funds. As a part of responsibility for fund acquisition and use, a system for analyzing fund flows is necessary. The emphasis on fund

Table 6-1: Identification of the Finance Functions

A. Specific Finance Areas

   1. Management of fund flows

      a. Effective acquisition of funds
      b. Efficient utilization of funds
      c. Analysis of fund flows
      d. Specification and monitoring of liquidity objectives or constraints

   2. Management of capital

      a. Management of the financing mix
      b. Utilization of capital budgeting concepts
      c. Analysis of decisions and actions affecting values
      d. Maximization of capital values

B. General Management Functions

   3. Management of information flows

      a. Formulation of a system of accounts to guide resource allocation
      b. Analysis of portfolio decisions

   4. Management of the planning and control process

      a. Analysis to set standards
      b. Formulation of alternatives, plans, and policies
      c. Periodic review of performance in comparison with plans
      d. Corrective actions and modification of plans
      e. Incentives system to reward and penalize performance in order to realize the firm's full potentials.

---

flows relates to the liquidity objectives or constraints that are a part of business policy.

The next set of functions relates to maximizing capital values. The marginal efficiency of investment function is related to the cost of capital function appropriately defined. The criteria for capital-budgeting and financing-mix decisions involve an analysis of all actions of the firm which may affect its capitalized value. It is in this context that the statement is sometimes made that finance is concerned with any decisions or actions of the firm which may influence its value. Therefore finance is responsible for the analysis of all alternative decisions or actions of the firm and has the purpose of selecting those decisions and actions that will lead to the maximization of the value of the ownership of the firm. It is for these reasons that section *2d* of Table 6-1 represents the maximizing capital value objective. Maximization of capital value is the prime objective and liquidity considerations (section *1d*) represents a constraint rather than an objective.

Information flows provide intelligence on the flows of funds, people and materials. The analysis of information flows is focused first on the formulation and operation of a system of accounts to guide efficient resource allocation. The criteria for evaluating the efficiency of a system of accounts regarding resource allocation must include the following:

1. Prompt information on the effects of decisions and actions.
2. Information that is relevant for the important and critical aspects of the firm's operations.
3. A system that provides visibility for a time-phasing of policies and actions. The time-phasing includes decisions and actions for improving day-to-day operations to a framework for effective planning of policies over extended time horizons.

Portfolio analysis   The second aspect of information flows is concerned with portfolio analysis. This includes information not only about maximum values for individual projects but also about their relationship to other projects. This provides information on expected returns, on variances, and on relations between opportunities. It provides for the evaluation of alternative combinations of investments or portfolio analysis. In addition, it permits the use of Bayesian decision analysis for applying subjective probabilities to the outcomes of alternative decisions and actions as well as to the degree of correlation between groups of decisions and actions. Portfolio decisions also include consideration of the utility preference functions of the decision makers or of those on whose behalf their decisions and actions are taken. Finally, in the set of four major areas of responsibility for financial managers are the functions of planning and control. Depending upon the background, abilities, and interests of the financial manager, his participation is likely to be of varying degree. By virtue of the authority of knowledge and interest, he may dominate the planning and control activities. At a minimum, he is likely to participate with the other top management executives.

In summary, the central responsibilities of the finance function relate to fund flows and the financing mix. In the performance of these functions, the financial manager is likely to have important responsibilities in connection with the evaluation of all decisions and actions affecting the value of the firm. Thus, the financial manager is likely to have the important responsibility of bringing together an analysis of capital budgeting and programs related to the determination of the amount and types of financing (the financing mix decisions). In addition, the financial manager is likely to perform an important role in the formulation of information flows. It also includes analyses related to portfolio decisions. Finally, finance bears an important relationship and responsibility to the broad planning and control activities in the firm, since these are critical for fund and resource allocation. But none of these activities of the financial manager should be viewed in a static orientation. The decisions of the financial manager are made in a firm whose nature and dynamic processes are undergoing

continuing change. In addition, the firm operates in an environment
in which significant, technological, sociological, political, and economic changes have taken place. The nature of these trends and their
impact on the finance function are considered in the following section.

Major Environmental Developments

The increased significance of financial decisions to the business
firm reflects important changes in their environment. These developments will be briefly enumerated, and, then, their significance for
business operations, and the finance function in particular, will be
noted. They are:

1. Rise of large scale business units
2. Growth of spending on research and development
3. Increased product and market diversification
4. Increased emphasis on growth
5. Accelerated progress in transportation and communication
6. Narrowing profit margins
7. Increased importance of tax considerations

Rise of Large Scale Business Units

Several factors have led to the increased size of business firms. The
total size of the economy itself has grown. The growth rate of the
United States economy in current dollars has averaged 5 to 6 per cent
per annum since World War II. At a 6 per cent growth rate, the
economy would double in 12 years. Since two decades have elapsed
following the end of World War II, a firm whose growth has kept
pace with the economy as a whole has had to quadruple its sales and
assets. Other factors causing business units to increase in size relate to
trends in the relative prices of the factors of production. A labor shortage occurred in the immediate post-war period because of the rapid
growth of the economy. The increase in the demand for labor during
the immediate post-war period pushed up wage rates. On the other
hand, capital goods industries, such as machine tools and industrial
machinery, experienced relatively moderate price increases. The terms
of trade between labor and capital shifted, leading to the substitution
of capital for labor. Capital intensive firms tend to be of larger size
than less capital intensive firms to achieve better utilization of the
equipment.

Another factor resulting in increased size is the formation of economic blocs among foreign countries. This gives business firms in
these countries larger markets for their products. As a consequence,
it can be predicted that the size of firms in the European Economic
Community, for example, will increase over the next ten or twenty

years. In addition, the economies of scale achieved by selling in the economic bloc area will enable such firms to compete more aggressively with the mass production industries of the United States in areas such as Europe, third countries, and the United States itself. This will stimulate mergers and other attempts to achieve further economies of scale by both United States firms and foreign firms.

What is the significance of this for the financial manager? As firms become larger, the job of running the operation becomes too big for any one man. There is increased pressure for the use of formal controls. Couple this with advances in information gathering, compiling, storing, processing, and retrieval, and we find that the function of information management in a business firm has increased importance. Furthermore, in the large enterprise the over-all operation is segmented into divisions, product lines, and profit centers. Thus, there may be a large number of profit centers in a business operation, and to plan and control a giant multi-division, multi-product operation requires increased responsibilities of the financial manager.

Growth of Spending on Research and Development

The increased pace of industrial research has accelerated the tempo of change in the economy. As a consequence, the necessity for planning and control has increased. When the tempo of change is hastened, the dangers of potential losses in "playing it by ear" are increased. If some firms plan and anticipate new opportunities, it gives them an advantage over those that do not. Furthermore, developments in both the theory and technique of planning and control have taken place. The advances that have been made and the increased adoption of new techniques by business firms as well as the increased body of literature describing them provide a foundation for further progress.

The Employment Act of 1946 was a pledge by the federal government to plan and to study the needs of the economy. To the extent that the economy might fall below full employment levels, the federal government pledged to make up the difference. This meant that business firms could more confidently plan on growth and rely on federal government actions to reduce instability in the economy. This, in turn, generated a mass of literature dealing with planning by the government and individual firms. Increased long-range planning activities have resulted. Here again, financial executives perform a highly significant role.

Increased Product and Market Diversification

With the tempo of technological change increased life cycles of individual products have been shortened. The pace with which new products have been introduced has increased. The pressure for decentralization, divisionalization, and controls has increased with more products and greater market diversification. Hence, the necessity for obtaining the advantages of decentralization and, yet, for retaining the controls of centralization is obvious.

Mr. Alfred P. Sloan, Jr., has described how the so-called "General Motors" type of planning and control evolved.[1] The decentralized divisions were given maximum independence over decisions made at the local level—manufacturing, distribution, service departments. On the other hand, responsibility for finance, research and development, and balance between individual product lines were achieved through central control by product committees and by corporate level management. But, even more significant, any decisions made by the divisions requiring funds allocations, whether at the operating level or related to such areas as research and development and finance, came under the supervision, review, and control of management at the corporate level. The great importance of finance in assembling information and providing for its flow from the divisions to the corporate level is emphasized in the Sloan narrative.[2]

Increased product and market diversification accelerate the pace at which new products are introduced and existing product lines become obsolete. This multiplies the frequency with which problems may be faced by existing product lines. The necessity is increased for the kind of financial planning and control and monitoring of operations that come within the area of responsibility of finance. Thus, the central role of the return-on-investment analysis in planning and in evaluating performance—a financial technique—is highlighted. When a firm moves into highly diversified areas, the kind of intimate, direct supervision that management formerly could provide is lost. Such a firm must, therefore, exercise financial controls and becomes in part an investment company in its approach. It substitutes a complex of financial controls for direct management review of operations.

Increased Emphasis on Growth

How does increased emphasis on growth affect the financial manager? As sales grow, there is an increase in the amount of assets that have to be financed. The faster the rate of growth of the firm, the less likely it is that financing can be achieved from internal sources. Thus, the need for financing from external sources is increased as a consequence of the greater emphasis on growth.

---

[1] Alfred P. Sloan, Jr., *My Years with General Motors* (New York: Doubleday and Co., Inc., 1964).

[2] *Ibid.*, Chap. 5.

Accelerated Progress in Transportation and Communication

Today, any part of the world is only a few hours distant by jet travel. In less than a second, communication can be achieved by radio. Thus, all the countries of the world are closer together. While it was possible for some nations to stagnate for hundreds of years, the more recent influence of cultural contacts has stimulated change in all of the countries of the world. The emerging nations of Africa, Southeast Asia, and Latin America are seeking to accomplish in one generation what the nations of Western Europe and the United States took over a hundred years to achieve in terms of economic development. American firms will participate increasingly in the explosive international environment. Another type of financial planning and control will be required for the international market. The financial manager of the future may start his day deciding whether to raise money in the capital markets of Paris, London, Tokyo, or New York. He may consider the allocation of some of these funds to operations in Central America, Southeast Asia, or Africa. The scope of responsibility for obtaining and allocating corporate resources will be broadened.

The kinds of problems that will be faced will be different. An obvious one concerns multiple currencies. This involves taking into account changes in foreign exchange rates, dealing with restrictions on convertibility, and on the amounts and kinds of funds that can be raised in capital markets at different periods of time. Analysis is required of the relative advantage of the use of certificates of deposits in the local money markets in relationship to yields that can be obtained on treasury bills as compared with the federal funds market, and the use of the Eurodollar market in Western Europe and other kinds of foreign funds markets that will develop. Obviously, the financial manager of the future is going to face a wide range of very sophisticated money market choices.

Narrowing Profit Margins

In a developed nation, such as the United States, many industries are in the mature phase of their life cycle. As industries reach the saturated phase of the life cycle, sales-to-capacity relationships become less favorable, profit margins narrow and decline, increased pressures for cost control develop.

With a large volume of output, the industry has thus reached the stage where the saving of a half-cent per unit may make the difference between being a successful or an unsuccessful competitor. Obviously, the role of finance in devising financial control systems and in monitoring them takes on major importance. With narrowing profit margins, there is increased pressure for new products, diversification, mergers—all devices aimed at moving the firm on to the new product life cycle at a more favorable stage or phase. Again, an increased role and importance for financial management is indicated.

Increased Importance of Tax Considerations

It can be stated as a theorem that tax laws are never simplified. To reform a tax code means changing the rules of the game for one group as compared to another group. Given the democratic process by which the Ways and Means Committee of the House of Representatives and the Finance Committee of the Senate hear a long list of witnesses whenever any tax change is contemplated, the amount of tax reform or simplification that can be accomplished as a practical matter is not large. Thus, the whole history of tax change is to superimpose each new tax law on the preceding old law. Furthermore, since any change may increase taxes for some groups, relief is always likely to be sought. More and more special interest groups come to Congress to ask that the tax law be changed, because it bears harshly on their particular group. Also, the tax laws are becoming more complicated because of special bills and provisions that are passed. The number of such proposals presented to the House Ways and Means Committee during recent sessions of Congress numbered in the hundreds.

Any decision regarding product planning and choice of forms of financing, involves a pattern of income or expense flows and has tax implications. Entire departments of large firms are now devoted to developing an expertise on this aspect of business operations. Tax departments as well as labor, fixed plant and equipment, and stockholders have a role of central importance in the operation of the business firm. It is an aspect of operations in which the financial executive has obviously an important responsibility.

Implications of Emerging Trends

As a consequence of these fundamental trends developing in the economy, the role of the financial manager is continuing to evolve, as is evidenced in the following statement:

> The complications introduced into business life by these changes have obliged many corporations to turn for guidance to men who understand the complications. And so many financial officers have a greatly broadened set of responsibilties. They include not only financing and controlling the company, but analyzing and interpreting the economic situation, appraising managerial performance, negotiating acquisitions and mergers, maintaining credit lines with banks, holding the good

opinion of the investing public, and, in fact, helping to set just about any of the policies that determine the company's future.[3]

In the context of the developing economic environment, the central functions of finance that have been defined are likely to take on great significance. These functions are:

1. Organizing a flow-of-information system to contribute to the efficient use of enterprise resources.
2. Effective management of fund flows.
3. Participation in the important planning and control process of the firm.
4. Participation in analysis of suboptimization decisions of divisions and groups and putting them together into over-all optimization for the business enterprise.
5. Responsibility for the physical aspects of the data flow and the use of new instruments, such as computers, in the record keeping and analytical activities of the business enterprise.

The impact of the emerging trends described above gives increased importance to the performance of the functions outlined. There is no inherent reason why all of these functions should be necessarily performed by financial officers. Where education, experience, ability, and interests of the financial officer lead him to participate actively in carrying out these functions, his role is likely to take on new power and importance. On the other hand, where all of these elements are not present, his role may become less important. The nature of the finance function, therefore, is likely to continue to evolve with the changing environment of the future.

The effect of these emerging trends upon the nature of the finance function has been well expressed as follows:

> Today the financial function has been further expanded and embraces such additional responsibilities as profit forecasting, establishing standards for costs and working capital, assisting top management in measuring business performance, and interpreting the operating results for all other management levels. The modern responsibilities of the chief financial officer necessarily involve him in the requirements and performance of virtually every phase of corporate activity. These responsibilities not only make him a potent factor in developing sound corporate planning, coordination and control, but they make it inevitable that he assume a leading role in the newer developments of the financial function. His work must be integrated into the overall marketing, production, and research plans.[4]

---

3 "The New Power of the Financial Executives," *Fortune,* January, 1962, pp. 81, 85.

4 Neal J. Dean, "Looking Ahead: New Developments, New Tools," *The Financial Manager's Job* (New York: American Management Assn., Inc., 1957), p. 444.

This statement admirably describes the evolution of the finance function and the possibilities of its future role. The emphasis on integration with other operating activities is a sound one. This emphasis on integration, if continued, would result in a total systems approach to business operations, as suggested earlier.

Financial Decision Areas

In this review of the environmental trends and their impact on the finance function, it is clear that the role of finance becomes increasingly significant. Finance must tie in closely to over-all management planning and control. This involves the establishment of (a) over-all profit goals, (b) departmental and division goals, (c) measuring progress and results against standards, and (d) action and adjustments to keep the company moving toward its goals and objectives. In describing the fundamental trends taking place in the environment and their impact on financial responsibilities, the central decisions of financial management were suggested. These decisions may now be made explicit in relation to the central kinds of generic responsibilities that have just been described in terms of efficient utilization of funds and resources. Let us consider some of these central questions for financial management.

1. How large should the enterprise be?
2. What growth rate should the enterprise seek in terms of sales, assets, employees, and profits?
3. What degree of stability should the enterprise seek?
4. What kinds of instability should it seek to avoid?
5. What kinds of assets should the firm acquire and at what rate?

These questions relate to the size and the rate of growth of the firm. Here, then, we must take into consideration some important subquestions.

1. What liquidity should the firm seek to achieve? A firm must always balance investment in real assets, inventories, and receivables against available cash or the opportunity of increasing the amount of cash. Liquidity relates to building up good financing relationships for the firm so that if the need for increased liquidity arises, the firm has some flexibility in achieving it.

2. Investment decisions are necessary with regard to all of the assets on the balance sheet of the firm. With regard to investment in receivables, what credit policy should the firm pursue? What terms of credit should be provided? Should collection policies be rigorous or moderate? To what extent should credit policies be tied to sales policies, and, hence, to a trade-off between price, to terms of delivery, or to collection policy?

3. Inventory investment decisions must be made. Should the firm purchase or manufacture an item? What degree of variability can be allowed in the amount of inventory items carried? What criteria for diversity and amounts of inventories should be followed? How should the level of inventories carried be related to the nature of the production process in the firm?

4. What should be the policy of the firm with regard to fixed assets? Should the firm lease or purchase? What expected life of assets should be emphasized? Should the firm purchase specialized or general purpose assets? Which fixed assets should the firm purchase and which should it manufacture?

All of the preceding questions relate to the kinds of assets, their size, and growth rate. Balance sheets reflect different degrees of owned versus purchased, manufactured versus bought, specialized versus general assets. The need to purchase assets is related to the products the firm shall sell. In what markets should the firm operate? The wide range of product-market decisions is related to the asset composition of the balance sheet. These questions involve the fundamental, strategic, long-range planning decisions of the firm.

Next is a whole series of questions on how the assets of the firm should be financed—the traditional questions of business finance:

1. Should the terms of financing be of short or long duration?
2. Should debt or equity financing be used?
3. What impact will this have on the profitability of the firm?
4. What impact will financial decisions have on variations of risks, incomes, controls, and claims of various sources of financing?
5. What options should be offered to investors to change the form of their claims under certain conditions?

When the variations in risk, income, control, claims, and various forms of options are taken into account, the possible product variations in forms of financing and sources of financing that could be devised run into the hundreds of thousands. This provides a rich, fertile, and challenging group of questions to confront the decision maker in the finance area.

The Nature of the Finance Function

It is clear that the scope of the finance function may be narrow or broad. In part, this depends upon the characteristics of the firm in which the financial manager is operating. In a technically oriented firm, the dominating executives may be technically oriented. In consumer non-durable goods industries, such as soap, food, and tobacco products, the importance of marketing and promotion may be so great that marketing executives may dominate the firm. Or, in any of these firms, the necessity for careful planning and control of operations may cause the financial manager to occupy a central position.

In addressing himself to his increased responsibilities, a wide range of tools are available to the financial officer. He will utilize the traditional tools of financial ratio analysis and budget systems, with particular emphasis on cash flows and cash budgets. In addition, financial projections, forecasts, and plans will be essential elements of the planning and control process. In addition, all of the techniques of modern operations analysis will be employed, including linear programming and quadratic programming. Furthermore, in developing judgments about the uncertain world, the principles of Bayesian statistics and subjective probability judgments will be employed. The elements of decision theory related to making consistent choices must also be included. Finally, in connection with the increased role of the computer, a systems approach may be taken to the entire enterprise activity. If the operations of the firm are viewed as a system with flows, there would tend to be a breakdown between the traditional functions such as production, marketing, and finance.

These may also develop a general command function that views all of the activities of the firm as part of a total system. In this role, the command function might take over analysis of information flows and record keeping for the analysis of fund flows. In such circumstances, the role of the financial officers might be limited to record keeping and acquisition and custody of funds. Indeed, if a systems approach is taken through the computer, record keeping would be performed by the manager of computer operations.

On balance, therefore, our conclusion about the nature of the finance function is conditioned by the facts of economic and business life. As the nature of business operations evolves in the future, and if information flows and analysis are taken over by a functionary, separate from that of financial officers, the finance function may diminish in importance to the acquisition and custody of funds. On the other hand, if information flows continue to be the major responsibility of finance, the finance role in enterprise activities will be magnified rather than reduced.

The Impact of Financial Decisions
on Economic Behavior

THE EVOLUTION of the nature of the finance function described in the previous chapters can be summarized into two themes. The emphasis on the acquisition of funds has been broadened into analysis of all aspects of the effective utilization of those funds—efficient business resource allocation. The preoccupation with the description of the instruments and institutions of finance has been broadened into analytical tools for evaluating the consequences of decisions (choices between alternatives) in the acquisition and utilization of funds. These developments have in turn had an impact on economics. In the present chapter, the implications of financial decisions on economic behavior are analyzed. The following chapter suggests the impact of new developments in financial theory on economic theory.

Financial Decisions and Investment Behavior

A gap between the subject of capital budgeting in business finance and the economic theory of investment has long existed. From capital budgeting decisions it would be presumed that the nature of the marginal efficiency of investment schedule would be developed. The cost of capital discussion should be relevant for an understanding of the supply of funds. The gap has existed for reasons on both sides.

Until recently, business finance had not explicitly developed propositions about capital budgeting and the cost of capital. The failure of economics to consider business finance has been well stated by Professor Gordon.

> For a long time the theory of finance lay dormant as a neglected subdivision of the theory of investment. The reason for this is of some interest. The investment of a firm according to traditional theory is determined by consideration of the marginal efficiency of capital employed in the firm and the cost of capital. The concern of finance is the source of funds to finance the investment-debt, retained earnings, or new equity funds, but as Hart stated, "On the assumption of a perfect and purely competitive capital market, each firm is confronted with a market rate of interest at which it can get all the capital financing it chooses." Finance is no problem in this case. So much of the theory of investment has proceeded on the above assumption of perfect capital markets that not a few economists have looked on the problem of finance as being of little or no consequence in fact.[1]

Thus, if the economist assumes a perfect and purely competitive capital market, each firm is presented with a perfectly elastic supply of funds schedule. In such an approach there is no distinction between cost of equity funds and the cost of debt funds. Economists writing about relationships between the marginal efficiency of investment schedule and the supply of funds simply refer to interest costs. The crucial questions of the debt versus equity mix are not treated, nor is there any recognition of the interest rate structure. Moreover, no distinction is made between instruments of differing maturities or of different qualities. Yet, in other specialized studies of economics, and particularly in empirical studies of investment behavior, the financial policies of firms are recognized to perform a role.

> Along side of and largely independent of the above theoretical work, empirical work by Merwin, Mack, Heller, Butters and Lintner, Meyers and Kuh, and others has established quite conclusively that internally available funds and attitudes toward debt have considerable influence on the investment behavior of firms.[2]

The empirical studies of investment behavior bring into consideration factors such as liquidity, leverage, and the availability of internal funds. Professor Cooper stated these matters in the following terms:

> A case might be made, it would seem, for analyzing the effect of the cash position of these "firms." In particular, a case might be made for analyzing the relation between cash position and control retention—or, more generally, between liquidity, profit, and control.

---

[1] Myron J. Gordon "Security and a Financial Theory of Investment," *The Quarterly Journal of Economics,* LXXIV (August, 1960), p. 472.
[2] *Ibid.,* p. 473.

Such analyses might also throw considerable light on oligopoly behavior and the conditions under which "discipline" can be maintained. It seems reasonable to expect that when cash position has deteriorated to where control of the individual firm by the entrepreneur is imperiled, quite different behavior patterns may emerge than when cash position and control retention are "secure."

One of the characteristics that distinguishes top- from lower-echelon management is the problem of administering the equity accounts—of so arranging the corporation's assets as to be able to meet impending claims and avoiding bankruptcy. Down-the-line management has virtually no contact with these problems. Neither "meeting next Thursday's pay roll" nor arranging financing is their immediate concern. It is in this direction that control retention lies. Put somewhat differently, control retention frequently involves questions of reconciliation between profit-and-loss statement and balance-sheet considerations.

Turning to strictly theoretical aspects, it might be said that economics has at least two theories of the firm: the banking firm and the business firm. With slight exaggeration, it may be said that the theory of the business firm is presented entirely from the profit-and-loss statement point of view, while the bank is analyzed in terms of its balance sheet. In one case, an elaborate paraphernalia of cost and demand curves serves as the foundation of analysis. Profit maximization reigns supreme. In the other case, this apparatus disappears. Attention is focused on balance-sheet position, and primary emphasis shifts to liquidity (reserve maintenance) considerations as a means of meeting equity commitments (deposits).[3]

Thus, Cooper years ago recognized liquidity, equity ratios, and control as balance sheet (financial policy) variables with important influences on income statement objectives. Indeed, wealth maximization requires consideration of both balance sheet (investment and financing) and income statement performance. The famous du Pont chart of financial control combines elements of both the income statement and balance sheet.

Professor Boulding emphasized the same factors in his concept of the "homeostasis of the balance sheet." [4]

The simplest possible short-run theory of the organism is the theory of "homeostasis," to use a term from physiology. This is the view that there is some "state" of the organism which it is organized to maintain, and any disturbance from this state sets in motion behavior on the part of the organism which tends to re-establish the desired state . . .

The simplest theory of the firm is to assume that there is a "homeostasis

3 W. W. Cooper, "Theory of the Firm: Some Suggestions for Revision," *The American Economic Review*, XXXIX (December, 1949), pp. 1205-7.

4 Kenneth E. Boulding, *A Reconstruction of Economics* (New York: John Wiley & Sons, Inc., 1950), pp. 24-34.

of the balance sheet"—that there is some desired quantity of all the various items in the balance sheet, and that any disturbance of this structure immediately sets in motion forces that will restore the status quo . . .

In fact the theory of the firm, and of the economic organism in general, has not developed along these lines, but along the line of static equilibrium theory of "maximizing behavior." The concept of the balance sheet, unfortunately, has not been employed to any extent in developing the static theory of the firm, so that as generally presented in the textbooks the firm is a strange bloodless creature without a balance sheet, without any visible capital structure, without debts, and engaged apparently in the simultaneous purchase of inputs and sale of outputs at constant rates. In spite of this weakness, much of the static theory of the firm can be salvaged and put into balance-sheet form: nevertheless, even when this has been done we still do not have a life-cycle theory, but only a theory of an equilibrium position of all the variables of the firm.[5]

These ideas of Boulding suggest a fuller development of the relations between output and price decisions and the effects on the balance sheet position of the firm. These concepts have, however, made little penetration. One limitation of the formulation is that the balance sheet position might better be considered as constraints on maximizing behavior rather than as goals of the enterprise.

Robin Marris has sought to integrate the corporate finance theory of the valuation of the firm into both microeconomic and macroeconomic theory.[6] His theory includes a discussion of market opportunities related to the growth of turnover (sales), internal profitability rates, the gearing (leverage) ratio, and the retention ratio. Space does not permit a systematic summary of the many stimulating ideas presented. Some of the findings of the work may be implied by Marris' observation that his results are similar to those of Myron Gordon in his analysis of a similar set of factors.[7]

In addition, all the studies on credit standards, credit terms, and quality of credit suggests the influence of financial variables. Credit standards refer to an appraisal of characteristics of borrowers employed by lenders. Very important in the definition of credit standards in the writings on the subject are the existing liquidity and leverage positions of the borrowers. Credit terms refer to the ratio of loan to security that may be provided by the lender and the requirements imposed by the lender as to the maturity of the loan, the repayment schedule, and liquidity and leverage standards that the borrower must main-

---

[5] *Ibid.*, pp. 24-34.

[6] Robin Marris, *The Economic Theory of "Managerial" Capitalism* (New York: The Free Press of Glencoe, Inc., 1964).

[7] Myron J. Gordon, *The Investment, Financing and Valuation of the Corporation* (Homewood, Ill.: Richard D. Irwin, Inc., 1962).

tain for the duration of the financial contract. Furthermore, the whole subject of financing of small firms reflects a recognition of the role of financing. Small firms are said to operate at a disadvantage compared to larger firms.[8] The numerous writings about the handicaps of the small firm with respect to financing are acknowledgments that the supply of funds is not a perfectly elastic function regardless of the situation or policies of the borrower.

If the analysis of investment decisions in the firm takes into account liquidity, leverage, credit standards, credit terms, and the size of the firm, implicitly the gates are open to a consideration of the full range of financial policy variables. The analysis must then consider internal versus external financing, the debt versus equity mix, and other aspects of liquidity and leverage policies. Analytically, therefore, the theory of investment of the firm requires analysis both of demand and supply functions. In analyzing the investment decisions of the firm, the demand function characteristically represents some variant of the marginal efficiency of investment schedule. This aspect of the analysis can be incorporated into traditional marginal productivity theory.

Turning to the supply side, we must formulate a theory about the behavior of the supply schedule of funds for the business firm. If financial policy or the financing mix affects the supply schedule of funds, then the resulting equilibrium price will be affected. Thus, if the supply schedule of funds is a relevant factor, theories of investment behavior in turn must take financial variables into account. Financial variables would then affect investment decisions of the firm and would affect the theory of the growth of the firms.

Capital Budgeting and the Investment Function

The preceding section has raised a number of issues with regard to the relation between business finance topics and investment behavior. This relation is now analyzed in a systematic fashion.

Standard business finance discussion of capital budgeting treats four approaches to criteria for investment decisions. The four criteria are:

1. The cash payback period
2. The average return on investment
3. The internal rate of return
4. The present value method

Since the details of these methods are now discussed in standard business finance texts, this treatment will focus primarily on the implications of the capital budgeting criteria for the shape of the investment function. Myron Gordon has demonstrated that the rela-

---

[8] Edith Tilton Penrose, *The Theory of the Growth of the Firm* (New York: John Wiley & Sons, Inc., 1959), pp. 218-20.

tionship between the first three criteria for capital budgeting decisions depends upon the length of the payoff period designated by the investment decision maker and the actual period over which net cash flow of savings from the investor is realized.[9] Gordon shows that the main implication of the cash payback criteria is to set a very high investment hurdle rate where the payback period is as short as two or three years. The surveys indicate that the most widely used payback period is two to three years, and the impact of the use of the payback period may be illustrated by Figure VII-1.

In Figure VII-1, the investment function, labeled P, represents a marginal efficiency function reflecting the cash payback period. The function labeled i represents a marginal efficiency function based on the internal rate of return. It will be noted that the payback function is generally to the left of the marginal efficiency function based on the internal rate, it is also much less elastic. Thus, capital budgeting decisions based on the payback would be much less interest-elastic. In

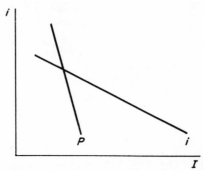

Figure 7-1.   Investment Functions

addition, the use of the payback period sets a much higher hurdle rate for investments than would a marginal efficiency function based on the internal rate of return. Thus, reliance on a cash payback capital budgeting decision rule would result in a lower volume of investment both for the firm and for the economy as a whole. Also, it is important to note that, regardless of the nature of the supply of funds schedule, investment is much less responsive under the payback criterion than under the use of the internal rate of return criterion.

The consequence of using the average investment formula estimate, likewise, is to set a relatively high investment hurdle rate, although generalization is difficult because the average investment estimate of

9 Myron J. Gordon, "The Payoff Period on the Rate of Profit," *Journal of Business,* October, 1955. Reprinted in Ezra Solomon (ed.), *The Management of Corporate Capital* (New York: The Free Press of Glencoe, Inc., 1959), pp. 50-51.

rate of return does not take the time value of money into account. Thus, the calculation of the average investment rate of return depends upon the time pattern over which cash outlays are incurred and cash inflows are received. The marginal efficiency functions in economic studies are essentially based on the internal rate of return. This has been spelled out by Armen A. Alchian in another article reprinted by Ezra Solomon.[10] Professor Alchian argues that the Fisherian rate of return over cost produces results equivalent to Keynes' internal rate of return.

The present value method can also be presented in a marginal efficiency function. The present worth approach avoids disadvantages of other methods. When cash outflows are incurred after a series of positive cash inflows, the calculation of the internal rate of return may result in dual rates of return.[11] Thus, each of the four capital budgeting criteria from business finance is reflected in the position and slope of the marginal efficiency of investment function. Since the marginal efficiency function represents a demand for capital goods, the shape and position of the function will have important implications for the rate of investment by the firm, as well as for the rate of aggregate investment in the economy.

As is shown in Figure VII-2 the Keynesian marginal efficiency of investment function differs in two respects from those that have been exhibited thus far. First, investment is a function not only of the interest rate but also of the level of national income. This is indicated in the figure by the position of the two investment functions. The investment function labeled Y_u represents the investment schedule during a business upswing. It lies to the right of Y_b, representing an investment function for a period during a business downswing. The second difference is that Y_b is relatively interest inelastic, whereas Y_u is relatively elastic with respect to the interest rate. Thus, during a business downswing, for a given interest rate level, the amount of investment for Y_b will be much smaller than the amount of investment for the Y_u schedule. In addition, for a given lowering of the interest rate schedule from i_0 to i_1, the increase in investment with the schedule Y_b is much smaller than the increase in investment for the schedule Y_u.

The Keynesian marginal efficiency of investment schedule suggests that the business firms' estimates of future savings or cash inflows from investment projects are calculated more optimistically during a business upswing than during a business downswing. In addition, all

10 Armen A. Alchian, "The Rate of Interest, Fisher's Rate of Return over Costs and Keynes' Internal Rate of Return," *The American Economic Review*, December, 1955. Reprinted in Ezra Solomon (ed.), *The Management of Corporate Capital* (New York: The Free Press of Glencoe, Inc., 1959), p. 67.

11 J. Hirshleifer, "On the Theory of Optimal Investment Decision," *Journal of Political Economy*, August, 1958. Reprinted in Ezra Solomon, Editor, *The Management of Corporate Capital* (New York: The Free Press of Glencoe, Inc., 1959).

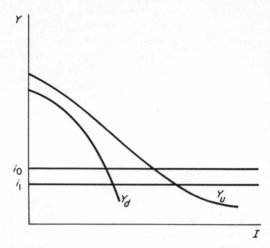

Figure 7-2.   Cyclical Shifts in Investment Functions

of the other factors which potentially may influence the level of investment are likely to function with unequal impact during a downswing as compared with an upswing. The analysis by Meyer and Kuh and the extensive studies by Eisner and Strotz indicate that a wide range of variables influence investment decisions.[12] Some of these relations are indicated in Table 7-1. During a business upswing, when previous peak capacity is expected to be exceeded, the accelerator goes into operation. Expectations of increased volume of sales will put the accelerator in gear and generate increased investment. The expectation of increased sales is also likely to be positively correlated with an expected high rate of return on such investments and will, thus, be correlated with sales increases and profitability increases. During a business downturn when excess capacity exists, liquidity conditions may play an increased role. Hence, an increased percentage of investments will be associated with new products or cost reduction.

This analysis of the implications of capital budgeting criteria for the nature of the investment function supports the following conclusions. (1) Alternative capital budgeting criteria are likely to influence the shape and position of the investment function. (2) The position and shape of the investment function are influenced by the expected level of national income and expected changes in national income. (3) At different levels of economic activity, the investment func-

[12] John R. Meyer and Edwin Kuh, *The Investment Decision* (Cambridge, Mass.: Harvard University Press, 1957).

Robert Eisner and Robert H. Strotz, "Determinants of Business Investment," in *Impacts of Monetary Policy*, a report prepared for the Commission on Money and Credit (Englewood Cliffs, N.J.: Prentice-Hall, Inc., 1963), pp. 59-337.

Table 7-1: Summary Table of Empirical Findings: Relative Importance of Investment Variables

VARIABLES / CONDITIONS	Interest Rate	Profits	Sales	Liquidity	Depreciation Res.	External Funds	Capacity Acceleration	Durability of Capital	Capital Labor Costs
General	negative				counter-cyclical			insignificant	insignificant
Big Firm						important	more important than small firm		
Small Firm		important		important	important	very important	important		
Growing Firm				not important		important	important		
Aged Firm		negative with age		important	important				
Inflation				not important	not much influence		important		
Non Infl.				important	important				
Long Run			important over profit			important	important		
Short Run		important		important					
Others		important when liquidity falls		pre-requisite for capacity expansion	correlated with age				

Stock prices: reflection of firm performance which, in turn, becomes an important dynamic variable for investment behavior.

Source: John R. Meyer and Edwin Kuh, *The Investment Decision* (Cambridge, Mass.: Harvard University Press, 1957).

tion reflects a wide range of other factors. We next turn to an analysis of the cost of capital function and its implications.

The Cost of Capital Function and Investment Decisions

One of the central decision areas of business finance is choice of financing mix. The choice of financing mix is relevant for investment decisions, because it influences the shape and position of the supply of funds function. This is the reason why we now analyze the cost of capital function to complete the basis for an analysis of investment decisions by bringing together both the demand and supply aspects. Three major types of theories of the shape and position of the cost of capital function have been advanced. They are: (1) the sequential cost of capital function of Duesenberry, (2) the perfectly elastic cost of capital function of Modigliani and Miller and (3) the U-shaped cost of capital function of traditional business finance. The implications of each of these will be considered.

The Duesenberry Sequential Source of Funds Approach

Professor Duesenberry has suggested that the cost of capital function has a relatively elastic initial segment, then a relatively inelastic segment as the quantity of funds which the firm seeks to raise becomes large. Duesenberry has expressed the rationale for this cost of capital function as follows:

> If we plot the imputed cost of investable funds against the rate of investment with fixed retained earnings and profits, we get a schedule like the one in Figure 8 [see Figure VII-3], where the imputed cost of funds is measured on the vertical axis and the rate of investment plus initial debt on the horizontal axis. The schedule is perfectly elastic, or nearly so, at a relatively low rate of return until $I + D$ equals depreciation expense plus retained earnings. It then rises, at first slowly and then steeply as investment plus initial debt increases. When imputed cost of debt rises so high that equity issues are justified, the slope is reduced again. To obtain a schedule of investable funds for a particular year, we move the origin to the right by an amount equal to the firm's initial debt and consider only a limited range of the schedule.[13]

One of the aspects emphasized by Duesenberry is that the shape of the cost of capital function has a significant influence on the level and variations in the amount of investment. Thus, if the marginal efficiency

---

13 James S. Duesenberry, *Business Cycles and Economic Growth* (New York: McGraw-Hill Book Company, Inc., 1958), pp. 96-97. This formulation is also employed in R. Lindsay and A. W. Sametz, *Financial Management, An Analytical Approach* (Homewood, Ill.: Richard D. Irwin, Inc., 1963).

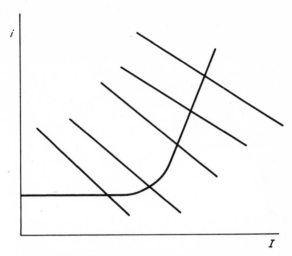

Figure 7-3.   Duesenberry's Cost of Capital Function

of investment function should intersect the cost of capital in its in-elastic range, investment will not be responsive to changes in the level of interest rates. Duesenberry states the relationship as follows:

> In periods of high prosperity many firms will be operating in the in-elastic range of their supply-of-funds schedule. As long as they do so, limited variations in the marginal-efficiency-of-investment schedule, whether due to expectations or other factors, will have little influence on the rate of investment.[14]

The full implications of this suggested shape of the cost of capital function by Duesenberry have been developed by Professor Kuh in the following terms:

> Hence, even if the marginal-efficiency-of-capital schedule is highly returns-elastic (which Duesenberry argues to be the case), variations in the cost of funds will have small effect on the firm's rate of investment because, the marginal efficiency schedule is "trapped" in the steeply rising range of the firm's cost-of-capital schedule. This provides a ration-alization for paying slight attention to capital costs, which Duesenberry quite rightly shows to be very different from market rates of interest.[15]

The quotation from Kuh brings in two elements. One is that re-gardless of the shape of the marginal efficiency function, it may be "trapped" in the steeply rising section of the firm's cost of capital schedule. Thus, even if the marginal efficiency function becomes highly

14 *Ibid.*, p. 111.
15 Edwin Kuh, *Capital Stock Growth: A Micro-Econometric Approach* (Amster-dam: North-Holland Publishing Company, 1963), p. 51.

interest elastic, as suggested by Keynes (illustrated in Figure VII-2 with the schedule Y_u), the rate of investment will not be responsive to interest rate changes. The second element brought in by Kuh is that capital costs must reflect the mix of internal financing, equity financing, and debt, not just the market rate of interest on debt. Figure VII-3 suggests that when the cost of capital is intersected at its relatively inelastic section, the amount of investment is determined by the position of the marginal efficiency function. It is in this sense that the rate of interest has little influence on investment decisions at this segment of the cost of capital function.

The diagram suggests a number of other relationships as well. The liquidity position, or the availability of internal funds, influences the quantity of investment level at which the cost of capital function begins to rise sharply and becomes interest rate inelastic. It also illustrates why the retention rate of a growing firm is likely to be very high (its dividend payout will be relatively small). The firm seeks to prolong the relatively horizontal section of its cost of capital function.

The point at which the cost of capital function shifts from a relatively horizontal segment to a relatively vertical segment occurs when the firm is forced to seek external financing. A small amount of external debt financing will probably have little impact on the firm's cost of capital function. When the debt ratio begins to rise, however, the cost of capital will then rise, reflecting the increased risk to creditors. At some point, the debt ratio becomes so high that the firm finds it necessary to seek external equity financing. At this point the cost of capital rises sharply. Despite the fact that the mix of equity and debt financing can then be proportioned to satisfy whatever credit standards are imposed by suppliers of funds, the total cost of capital function is still much higher because of the necessity of raising external funds, including some portion of equity funds.

Thus, at a certain range of growth on the part of individual firms, the availability of internal funds and liquidity may greatly influence the level of investment, particularly during that phase of the business cycle in which the marginal efficiency function is shifting to the right. After the marginal efficiency function has shifted to the right and begins to fall in the interest inelastic section of the firm's cost of capital function, the amount of investment no longer increases at the same pace that it did in the earlier stages of the cycle, and the rate of capital spending increases can, therefore, be expected to decline.

In addition, the diagram illustrates that interest rate policy which causes the cost of external funds to increase is likely to have little impact on the level of investment. It has little impact on the level of investment over the horizontal section of the cost of capital function because financing is mainly internal. When the cost of capital function reaches its sharply vertical section, the inelasticity of the function is so great that it swamps the impact of interest rate level changes.

There is a possibility, of course, that a change in interest rate policy would shift the horizontal schedule upward, but this is likely to have little impact on investment decisions for two reasons: (1) the marginal efficiency schedule is shifting to the right during this period, and (2) a change in monetary policy is not likely to take place until evidence of a high level of activity in the economy has become available, at which time the firm is already near the vertical segment of its cost of capital function.

In summary, the cost of capital function suggested by Duesenberry can potentially have an influence on the rate of investment and rates of change in investment. The actual impact of the change is an empirical matter. It depends upon movements of the marginal efficiency schedule in relationship to the cost of capital function. Regardless of one's evaluation of the conclusions drawn by Duesenberry and Kuh, their discussions indicate a number of possible configurations of relationships with implications for the rate and level of business investment. Regardless of the actual empirical relationships between movements of the marginal efficiency schedule and the shape and position of the cost of capital schedule, it is clear that a potential exists for the cost of capital function of the business firm which has significant implications for economic policy.

The Horizontal Cost of Capital Function of Modigliani and Miller

The Modigliani-Miller cost of capital function has been discussed at length in a number of places.[16] Figure VII-4 illustrates the

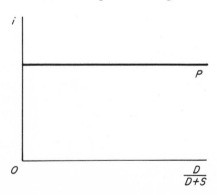

Figure 7-4. Modigliani-Miller Cost of Capital Function

---

[16] F. Modigliani and M. H. Miller, "The Cost of Capital, Corporation Finance and the Theory of Investment," *The American Economic Review*, June, 1958. Reprinted in Ezra Solomon (ed.), *The Management of Corporate Capital* (New York: The Free Press of Glencoe, Inc., 1959). For a brief evaluation see J. F. Weston, "A Test of Cost of Capital Propositions," *The Southern Economics Journal*, October, 1963, pp. 105-12.

Modigliani-Miller cost of capital function. The cost of capital, ρ , is the rate at which the net income stream on an unleveraged company is capitalized. This is also the over-all cost of capital for any firm in a given risk class. It will be noted that the horizontal axis of the Modigliani-Miller diagram differs from that of the Duesenberry diagram presented in Figure VII-3. The Duesenberry diagram has quantity of financing on the horizontal axis with the composition of financing changing as the quantity of financing is increased. The Modigliani-Miller diagram has nothing directly on the quantity of financing obtained but deals only with the financial mix. Thus, it deals with a different set of problems than those suggested by the Duesenberry diagram of Figure VII-3.

Cost of Capital in Traditional Business Finance

The import of the Modigliani-Miller theory of the cost of capital is that decisions of the firm with regard to financing mix cannot affect the level or rate of real investment activity. This is in contrast to traditional business finance theory which postulates a U-shaped cost of capital function. With a U-shaped cost of capital function, as shown in Figure VII-5, financing mix decisions by business firms can influence the cost of capital. Traditional business finance says that there is an optional range of financing mix in which the cost of capital to

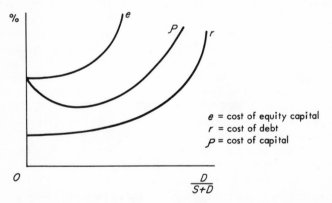

e = cost of equity capital
r = cost of debt
ρ = cost of capital

Figure 7-5.   Cost of Capital, Traditional Business Finance

the firm can be lower. For a given marginal efficiency function, the amount of investment would, thereby, be influenced.

Figure VII-6 brings together considerations both of quantity and of financing mix. The Duesenberry rising cost of capital function with financing is combined with the traditional business finance theory of a U-shaped cost of capital function in relation to financing mix. L_0 represents the low point of the range of the cost of capital in relationship to financing mix. It represents the relatively flat part of the U-shaped cost of capital curve. If the degree of leverage, as indicated by the L curves, is either too small (L_1, L_2, L_3) or too large (L_4, L_5, L_6), the cost of capital would be higher than that which would have been obtained for the optimal financing mix.

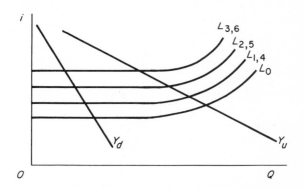

Figure 7-6. Supply and Demand for Funds

Thus, for a given marginal efficiency function, Y_d for example, the optimal financing mix would result in a somewhat higher rate of investment than for less optimal financing mix decisions. The impact on the amount of investment during a business upswing is likely to be substantially greater. In fact, this represents a plausible set of reasons why, when during a business upswing, the marginal efficiency function shifts to the right and becomes relatively interest-elastic, a change in business financing policy takes place. Under these circumstances, the businessman's aversion to debt is diminished. It diminishes for two reasons: (1) the risks of utilizing debt are diminished with more favorable income expectations, and (2) the strong pressure on capacity leads the businessman to seek ways of expanding plant capacity in order to maintain his share of the industry market.

Again, it is not intended in this discussion to argue that empirical data have established that one set of cost of capital functions is supported more convincingly than another. What the discussion does amply demonstrate is that differences in the possible shapes and positions of the cost of capital functions can have important impacts on the timing and rate of change in the level of investment activity, both for the individual firm and for the economy as a whole. Further implications for economic theory are developed in the following chapter.

```
8888888888888888888888888888888888888888888888888888888888888888888888888888888888888888
8888888888888888888888888888888888888888888888888888888888888888888888888888888888888888
888888888888888888888888    8888888888888    888    888    888    8888888888888888888888888
8888888888888888888888888    888888888888    8888    888    888    8888888888888888888888888
888888888888888888888888888    88888888    88888    888    888    8888888888888888888888888
88888888888888888888888888888    8888888    888888    888    888    8888888888888888888888888
8888888888888888888888888888888    88888    8888888    888    888    8888888888888888888888888
888888888888888888888888888888888    888    88888888    888    888    8888888888888888888888888
8888888888888888888888888888888888    8    888888888    888    888    8888888888888888888888888
88888888888888888888888888888888888        8888888888    888    888    8888888888888888888888888
888888888888888888888888888888888888    88888888888    888    888    8888888888888888888888888
8888888888888888888888888888888888888888888888888888888888888888888888888888888888888888
8888888888888888888888888888888888888888888888888888888888888888888888888888888888888888
```

The Impact of Developments in
Financial Theory on Economic Theory

THE TRENDS in the economic and technological environment have had
an impact on both business finance and economics. Some of the impacts on business finance have been treated in previous chapters. The
present chapter deals with some of the implications of developments
in financial theory for economic theory.

Integration of Price Theory and Capital Theory

For partial equilibrium analysis in economics, the factors determining the cost structure of the firm are not fully explored. The cost
functions for the individual firm in the partial equilibrium analysis
of the individual firm are given. Only their general shape in relation
to output variations is analyzed. In the construction of long-run cost
functions, selection of the scale of plant determines the firm's locus of
operations on its long-run cost curve. The elements of the capital investment decisions which lie behind the nature and shape of the
long-run average cost function, however, are not developed. Capital
theory is not integrated into the partial equilibrium theory of the firm.
The sections of economics books dealing with capital theory treat
the subject as a relatively independent body of material. The significance of capital theory for the pricing of final products or analyz-

ing the costs of factor inputs is not developed. The subject matter is treated in a brief and generalized manner. Illustrative of the basic approach to capital theory is the following quotation from the widely-used book by Samuelson.

> Related to the concept of the net productivity of capital is the important economic process by which capital goods get priced in the market at their "capitalized value." The interest rate plays a key role, and when the interest rate drops from a high to a low level, we shall see there must result a considerable rise in the capitalized value of machines, bonds, annuities, or any asset providing a stream of future property revenues.[1]

In such an approach to the theory of the firm and to capital theory, most of the subject matter of finance is neglected. This is not to say the material is not treated briefly. For example, some of the essentials of business finance are set forth in the Samuelson book. They are not related, however, to economics discussion in the other parts of the book. Their relevance or significance for decision making either for the firm or for the internal administration of the firm is not developed.

The increased pace of technological change has shortened product cycles and increased competition from new products. Profit maximization decisions for the short run must increasingly take recognition of capital investment planning. The profit maximization models must, therefore, be integrated into wealth maximization models.

Costs in Relation to Time, Rate, and Volume

An indication of how such integration might be achieved has been suggested by Alchian and Allen. They have analyzed costs in terms of volume, rate, and time period over which the output will come on to the market.[2] Since a number of years may be involved, they formulate costs in terms of the present value of total costs. The influence of both the differences of techniques, taking into account amounts and types of capital outlays, is indicated.

Figure VIII-1 reproduces an Alchian and Allen figure which illustrates, for automotive use, the relationship between technique of acquiring the use of autos and the capital value costs of operating them. The figure indicates that renting by the day is cheapest if the miles of service were very small. If, on the other hand, miles of service become larger, day-rent becomes very expensive. At moderate use,

---

[1] Paul A. Samuelson, *Economics: An Introductory Analysis* (New York: McGraw-Hill Book Company, Inc., 1961), p. 647.

[2] A. A. Alchian and W. R. Allen, *University Economics* (Belmont, California: Wadsworth Publishing Company, Inc., 1964), pp. 308-22.

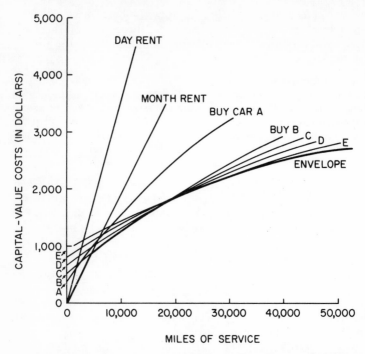

Figure 8-1.   Costs in Relation to Time, Rate and Volume

buying a car becomes cheaper after 10,000 miles of service a year. If the miles of service become as high as 50,000 miles a year, the least expensive way of financing the transportation sources may be to buy a total of five cars. This diagram illustrates that differences in the degree of capital commitment will influence the present value of cost per unit of output.

Output, Capital Requirements, and Present Value

Another approach which integrates price theory and capital value theory has been suggested by Lerner and Carleton.[3] Table 8-1 shows the structure of their system which contains a demand function, a cost function, a technological relation, and a profit function. The technological relation is critical, because it relates the conventional demand and cost functions to the size of the firm's assets and hence to capital theory as will be demonstrated.

The table provides an illustration of the relation between output

[3] Eugene M. Lerner and Willard T. Carleton, *A Theory of Financial Analysis* (mimeographed edition, 1965), Chapter V (Publication by Harcourt, Brace & World).

Table 8-1: Output Policy and Rate of Return

Demand: $P = a_0 + a_1Q$

$\qquad a_0 > 0; \ a_1 < 0$

Cost: $C = \beta_0 + \beta_1Q$

$\qquad \beta_0 \geqq 0; \ \beta_1 > 0$

Symbols: P = Price

$\qquad\quad Q$ = Quantity

$\qquad\quad A$ = Total Assets

$\qquad\quad \pi$ = Total Profits

Technological Relation:

$\qquad Q = \lambda \ A; \ \lambda = \text{Constant}$

Profits: $\pi = (P - C)Q$

$\qquad\quad \pi = a_0Q + a_1Q^2 - \beta_0Q - \beta_1Q^2$

$\qquad\quad \pi = (a_0 - \beta_0)Q + (a_1 - \beta_1)Q^2$

$\qquad\quad \pi = (a_0 - \beta_0)\lambda A + (a_1 - \beta_1)\lambda^2 A^2$

Rate of Return on Assets:

$$\frac{\pi}{A} = (a_0 - \beta_0)\lambda + (a_1 - \beta_1)\lambda^2 A$$

Change in Rate of Return on Assets $= \dfrac{\pi/A}{A} = (a_1 - \beta_1)\lambda^2 < 0$

---

policy and the rate of return. Here, the system taken from Table 8-1 is set forth and numerical parameters are provided for the equation system. A simple linear, negative sloping demand curve is postulated and a linear, positive sloping cost function. The technological relationship between output and assets is postulated at .05. The existence of the technological relationship permits profits to be expressed as a function of assets. The equation for profits, given these parameters, is:

$$\pi = 2A - .005A^2$$

The nature of the system may be observed at the maximum profit level. At the maximum profit level, marginal revenue equals marginal cost. Given the linear demand and supply functions, the marginal curves have slopes that are twice the slopes of the average revenue and average cost functions. The output that maximizes net receipts is a quantity of 10, at which the average revenue or price is $50, and the average cost per unit is $30.

Profit (average revenue minus average cost multiplied by quantity) can be obtained from the relationships just determined. Profit is ($50 − $30) times 10, yielding a total of $200. Given the quantity of 10 and the technological relationship between quantity and assets, we find that assets are $200 (by coincidence only equal to profits). We then place the value of A of $200 in the profit equation and confirm

Table 8-2: Illustration of Output Policy and Rate of Return

$$a_0 = 60$$
$$a_1 = -1$$
$$\beta_0 = 20$$
$$\beta_1 = 1$$
$$\lambda = .05$$
$$P = 60 - Q$$
$$C = 20 + Q$$
$$\pi = (P - C)Q$$
$$\pi = (a_0 - \beta_0)\lambda A + (a_1 - \beta_1)\lambda^2 A^2$$
$$\pi = (60 - 20).05A + (-1 - 1)(.05)^2 A^2$$
$$\pi = 2A - .005A^2$$

at maximum π,   *Test:*

$$MR = MC$$
$$MR = 60 - 2Q$$
$$MC = 20 + 2Q$$
$$20 + 2Q = 60 - 2Q$$

$$4Q = 40$$
$$Q = 10$$
$$P = \$50$$
$$C = \$30$$
$$\pi = (P - C)Q$$
$$\pi = (50 - 30)10$$
$$\pi = 200$$

$$Q = \lambda A$$
$$10 = .05A$$
$$A = \$200$$

$$\pi = 2A - .005A^2$$
$$\pi = 400 - .005(40,000)$$
$$\pi = 400 - 200$$
$$\pi = \$200$$

$$\frac{\pi}{A} = \frac{\$200}{\$200} = 100\%$$

$$\frac{\pi}{S} = \frac{\$200}{\$500} = 40\%$$

that profits are $200 at the optimal output of a quantity of 10. At this optimal output, profit is $200. The profit rate on total assets is 100 per cent, the profit rate on sales is 40 per cent. These are somewhat high ratios but not implausible for small firms. Furthermore, this provides a basis for illustrating the influence of turnover on the profit rate. These materials are provided in Table 8-3.

In Table 8-3 the influence of turnover on the profit rate is demonstrated. If $\lambda = .01$, A, given the quantity of 10, is $1,000. The profit function becomes $.4A - .002A^2$. At A of $1,000, the profit remains $200. This is to be expected, because profit is determined not by the size of assets but by the demand and supply functions. However, with a λ of only .01 and assets of $1,000, the profit rate on assets drops to 20 per cent. The profit rate on sales remains, however, at 40 per cent. Thus, the profit rate on total assets is a function of the turnover of total assets into sales. In Table 8-2, the turnover of assets into sales is 2.5, since sales are $500 and assets are $200. With assets of $1,000

Table 8-3: The Influence of Turnover on the Profit Rate

$$\text{If } \lambda = .01, \ A = \$1,000$$
$$\pi = (60 - 20).01A + (-2)(.01)^2 A^2$$
$$\pi = .4A - .0002A^2$$
$$\text{at } A = 1,000$$
$$\pi = 400 - 200$$
$$\pi = \$200$$
$$\frac{\pi}{A} = \frac{\$200}{\$1,000} = 20\%$$
$$\frac{\pi}{PQ} = \frac{\$200}{\$500} = 40\%$$

the turnover is only .5. Thus, with only a .5 turnover, the profit rate on assets drops to 20 per cent.

What is significant in this presentation by Lerner and Carleton is that by introducing the technological relationship, the quantity of output is linked to assets. Thus, a profit rate, r, or π/A is established, and output policy is related to the size of the firm's assets and, therefore, to the size of the capital investment. With this, the next step then is to use the profit rate in one of a number of standard financial capitalization formulas to link capital values to output policy. This will next be illustrated.

A widely accepted formula for the value of a perpetual income stream from an asset is:

$$P = \frac{D}{k - g}$$

where:

$P =$ the value of the asset

$D =$ the cash flow stream from the asset

$k =$ the capitalization rate

$g =$ the rate of growth in the perpetual income stream from the asset

By linking the quantity of output to the capital or assets required to produce the output, capital and output decisions are linked.[4] For example, the cash flow from the asset is Y. The cash flow to the in-

---

4 Some distinctions should be made clear. Capital budgeting procedures analyze returns from cash outflows and cash inflows. Accounting measures of net income differ from cash flows mainly in that depreciation expenses (a non-cash expense) are deducted. Accounting net income with depreciation added back is rough approximation to cash flows. Dividends paid by firms represent the current cash flows available to the equity investors.

vestor is D. The relation between the cash flow from the asset and cash flow to the investor may be expressed as:

$D = (1 - b) Y$, where b is cash flow retained in the enterprise.

But $rA = Y$; thus, the amount of capital or assets becomes a part of the relationship; therefore,

$$P = \frac{(1 - b)rA}{k - g} .$$

The scale of operations is reflected in A. For different sizes of capacity, the relation between quantity of output and A will vary. Thus λ may be regarded as a function of the size of A as well as the technology of the industry. Having chosen the optimum scale of operations for a planned range of output, the value of λ will be established. Given the scale of operations (specification of the short-run cost function and the place on the firm's long-run cost function), the output is chosen to maximize the firm's capital value, P.

It should be emphasized that in the present formulation the level of output which maximizes the firm's capital value is not necessarily the level of output which maximizes the firm's net receipts or net income stream, Y. The value of the firm is a function not only of the income stream, but also of the capitalization factor. As in break-even analysis, the larger the capital outlays and the higher, therefore, the fixed costs, the lower the variable costs are likely to be. At high levels of output permitted by the scale of plant thus decided upon, the profit of the capital-intensive firm will be higher. At low levels of output, the capital-intensive firm may suffer losses. These relations may be illustrated in standard break-even analysis, as shown in Figure VIII-2.

In this figure, the most capital intensive firm, Firm C, and the least capital intensive firm, Firm B, are shown. If output is 20,000 units, Firm C loses $40,000 and Firm B loses only $10,000. If the units sold are 120,000, however, Firm C earns a profit of $60,000 while Firm B earns a profit of only $40,000. Thus, the variability in the profits of Firm C is increased by its higher degree of operating leverage. The break-even volume of output sold for Firm C is 60,000 units while it is only 40,000 units for Firm B.

Since the variability of the net receipts for Firm C is much greater, investors may apply a higher capitalization rate, k, to the net cash flow from Firm C than to the net cash flow from Firm B. Thus, at a volume of 100,000 units, the net income stream from Firm C is $40,000, while the net income stream from Firm B is $30,000. Suppose the expected future growth rate from each is postulated to be the same, 4 per cent per annum. Because of the greater risk in Firm C, its earnings are capitalized at 8 per cent, while the earnings of Firm B are

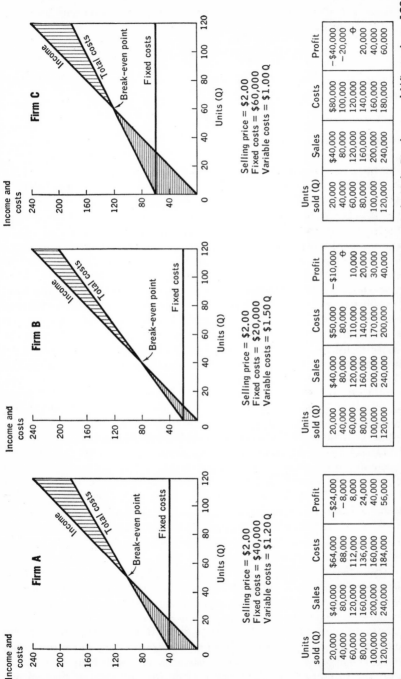

Firm A

Selling price = $2.00
Fixed costs = $40,000
Variable costs = $1.20 Q

Units sold (Q)	Sales	Costs	Profit
20,000	$40,000	$64,000	-$24,000
40,000	80,000	88,000	-8,000
60,000	120,000	112,000	8,000
80,000	160,000	136,000	24,000
100,000	200,000	160,000	40,000
120,000	240,000	184,000	56,000

Firm B

Selling price = $2.00
Fixed costs = $20,000
Variable costs = $1.50 Q

Units sold (Q)	Sales	Costs	Profit
20,000	$40,000	$50,000	-$10,000
40,000	80,000	80,000	φ
60,000	120,000	110,000	10,000
80,000	160,000	140,000	20,000
100,000	200,000	170,000	30,000
120,000	240,000	200,000	40,000

Firm C

Selling price = $2.00
Fixed costs = $60,000
Variable costs = $1.00 Q

Units sold (Q)	Sales	Costs	Profit
20,000	$40,000	$80,000	-$40,000
40,000	80,000	100,000	-20,000
60,000	120,000	120,000	φ
80,000	160,000	140,000	20,000
100,000	200,000	160,000	40,000
120,000	240,000	180,000	60,000

Figure 8-2. Operating Leverage. Source: J. F. Weston, Managerial Finance (New York: Holt, Rinehart and Winston), p. 198

capitalized at 6 per cent. We may insert these given data into the valuation formula for Firm C in P_C and for Firm B in P_B.

$$P_B = \frac{30,000}{.06 - .04} = \frac{30,000}{.02} = \$1,500,000$$

$$P_C = \frac{40,000}{.08 - .04} = \frac{40,000}{.04} = \$1,000,000$$

As the equations show, the indicated value of Firm B would be $1.5 million while the value of Firm C would be $1.0 million. Thus, the value of Firm B would be $500,000 more than the value of Firm C. Nevertheless, the indicated net receipts from Firm C are $40,000, or $10,000 more than for Firm B. This illustrates that the output which maximizes net receipts may not necessarily be the output which maximizes the value of the firm.

The foregoing example illustrates two major points. By relating output to assets required to produce that output, it shows the relationship between scale of operations (or capacity) and output, and, given the cost data, the cost of output per unit. In addition, the illustration emphasizes that the goal of maximizing net receipts may not provide the correct solution and indicates the rationale for maximizing present value as an objective.

Many other formulations could be devised to link capital theory and the analysis of output decisions for firms under competitive conditions and to price and output decisions for firms operating under conditions of imperfect competition. In fact, very little has been accomplished along these lines, although the most recent textbooks in economics begin to indicate an awareness of the problem. The foregoing illustration was developed only to be suggestive of the kinds of linkages that could be developed. As more work is done along these lines, the more complete will the integration of economic theory and finance theory be. These linkages at the level of the theory of the firm can also be extended to the theory of the behavior of the economic system. These relations are next considered.

The Total System for the Economy

The influences of the shape and position of the investment function reflect criteria for capital budgeting decisions. The cost of capital function is an important determination of the shape and position of the savings function. The shape and position of the marginal efficiency function, or investment function, and the shape and position of the cost of capital, or savings function, determine equilibrium in the capital market. This, of course, influences the equilibrium process in the total economic system. Every set of prices in capital, commodity, or factor markets must be consistent with the total economic system. Therefore, it may be of some value to see the relationship of the material we have been discussing in connection with prices in the capital markets to the operation of the total system.

Figure VIII-3 represents a graphical presentation of the operation of the total economic system. It represents an eclectic summary of the models that have been produced over a period of time by Modigliani, Lutz, Bailey, and generally reflected in the textbooks about macrotheory.

The capital market we have been discussing is portrayed in panel A of the figure. Given the shape and position of the marginal efficiency function and the savings function we have been discussing, equilibrium for a given level of income is established simultaneously in the capital market and in the money market. Given the demand for money which combines elements of liquidity preference and the transaction demand for cash, there exists an equilibrium rate of interest in the money market related to the supply of money. Equilibrium in this money and capital subsector must simultaneously determine the level of income, the demand for money, the supply of money, savings, investment, and the rate of interest. These six variables are determined by the functions of the capital and money markets, because these two diagrams represent the following six equations:

1. The supply of money equation.
2. The demand for money equation.
3. The equilibrium condition that the supply of money must equal the demand for money.
4. The investment function.
5. The savings function (and therefore, by implication, the consumption function).
6. The equilibrium condition that savings must equal investment.

We, thus, have six equations and six unknowns so that the six variables are simultaneously determined by the six-equation system.[5]

The conditions in the factor market are illustrated by panel C. A Keynesian labor supply function is illustrated with a horizontal section at a level institutionally determined and with a rising section when "full employment" is reached. Labor demand functions are illustrated as a function of money wages indicating money illusion both in the labor supply market and in the labor demand market. Money

---

[5] For a numerical illustration of how the six equations of the money and capital subsector simultaneously determine the six variables, i.e., demand for money, supply of money, income, the interest rate, investment, and savings, see J. F. Weston, "Models of the Pricing Process," in *The Relationship of Prices to Economic Stability and Growth: Compendium*, U.S. Congress Joint Economic Committee Document, No. 23734. (Washington: U.S. Govt. Printing Office, March 31, 1958), pp. 309-18.

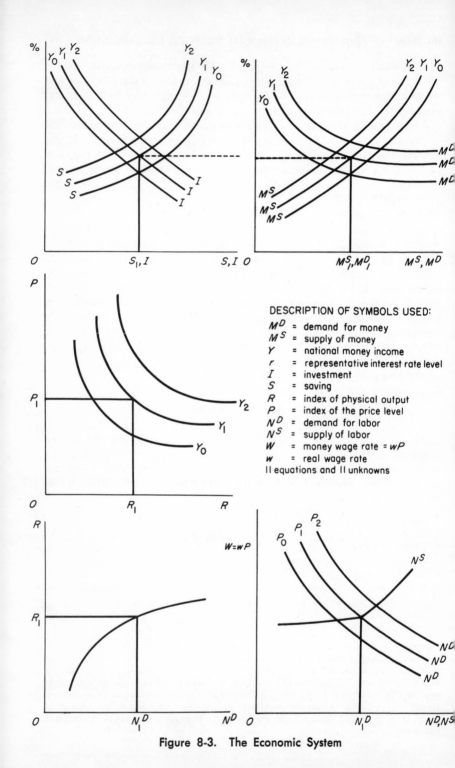

DESCRIPTION OF SYMBOLS USED:

M^D = demand for money
M^S = supply of money
Y = national money income
r = representative interest rate level
I = investment
S = saving
R = index of physical output
P = index of the price level
N^D = demand for labor
N^S = supply of labor
W = money wage rate = wP
w = real wage rate

11 equations and 11 unknowns

Figure 8-3. The Economic System

illusion in the labor market implies that both the demand and supply for labor are determined by money wages not by real wages. Thus, monetary policy can have an influence on the level of employment by altering the level of money wages.

The demand for labor function was determined by taking the first derivative of the production function exhibited in panel B. In the Keynesian system, equilibrium in the factor market (exhibited by panel C) and in the commodity market (exhibited by panel B) is not determinate until linked with the price level and money income functions exhibited in panel E. Money income is determined by equilibrium in the capital and money markets. Thus, given the relationship between real output, the price level, and money income exhibited by panel E, and given the production function of panel B and the value of money income from the money and capital subsectors, equilibrium in the factor and commodity subsectors is determined simultaneously. The complete system illustrated by the five panels is in full equilibrium. It is clear that the shape and position of the investment function and the cost of capital and savings functions will have influences throughout the complete economic system. Conversely, equilibrium in the capital markets will be influenced by the shape and position of functions appearing in each of the other four subsectors of the economy.

Finance and Models of Economic Growth [6]

The role of the financial mechanism is equally important in models illustrating the theory of economic growth. The role of the financial mechanism may be introduced by starting with the Harrod-Domar Model. In the Harrod-Domar Model, the following assumptions are involved:

1. One good,
2. Used for consumption or as capital input in production,
3. Labor only other input,
4. Constant returns to scale,
5. No technical progress,
6. Fixed technical coefficients of production,
7. A constant proportion (s) of income (Y) is devoted to savings,
8. The labor force grows at a constant rate (n), fixed by non-economic (demographic) forces.

---

[6] The following discussion of growth models in this section has benefited greatly from the lucid exposition of F. H. Hahn and R. C. O. Matthews, "The Theory of Economic Growth: A Survey," *The Economic Journal*, LXXIV (December, 1964), pp. 779-902. See also, J. F. Weston, "Influences of Stages of Development on Growth Rates," *Proceedings of the 1961 meetings of the American Statistical Association* (May, 1962), pp. 62-73. Both articles also contain numerous references to the relevant literature.

The resulting model operates as follows. Since the labor requirements per unit of output are given, national income (Y) cannot permanently grow faster than the growth rate in the labor force (n). Thus, n is the natural rate of growth defined as the highest rate of growth that is permanently maintainable. The warranted rate of growth (g_w) is defined as the equilibrium rate of growth. For an equilibrium rate of growth, the amount of planned saving (S) must equal the amount of planned investment (I). Also, the capital stock must grow at the same rate as output, which is to say that I/S must equal the rate of growth of income, which may be expressed as dY/dt. Equilibrium conditions are provided by the following relationship:

$$g_w = \frac{I}{K} = \frac{I}{Y} \cdot \frac{Y}{K} = \frac{s}{v}$$

where:

$$s = \frac{S}{Y}$$

$$v = \frac{K}{Y}$$

Thus, the capital stock growth is defined as I/K. Dividing the numerator and denominator by Y provides I/Y which is the investment rate out of income. For equilibrium, I/Y must be equal to the savings rate, or s, in the numerator of the final expression. This is multiplied by Y/K (the reciprocal of the capital-output ratio v) appearing in the denominator. We have thus derived the well-known Harrod-Domar determinants of the warranted rate of growth—the ratio of savings to the reciprocal of the capital-output ratio. This expression may also be illustrated by numerical coefficients plausible for the United States economy.

$$g_w = \frac{72}{1800} = \frac{72}{600} \cdot \frac{600}{1800} = \frac{12\%}{3} = 4\%$$

Thus, with investment of $72 billion, national income of $600 billion and a capital of $1.8 trillion, the savings rate would be 12 per cent and the capital output ratio would be 3. This would result in a warranted rate of growth for the economy as a whole of 4 per cent.

Steady state growth requirements imply the following equalities.

$$g_w = n, \quad g = \frac{s}{v} \quad \text{and} \quad n = \frac{s}{v} \quad v = \frac{s}{n} \quad \frac{n}{s} = \frac{1}{v}$$

Since n, s, and v are all independently determined, the steady state equilibrium conditions will be possible only in a special case. In other words, the equation system is overdetermined. We have one equation and no variables because n, s, and v are all given independently and exogenously. Thus, the equilibrium conditions will be achieved only by a fortuitous combination of unusual circumstances. This leads Harrod-Domar to conclude that, in general, full employment-steady growth is not attainable. To obtain a steady-state growth model, at least one of the critical influences among n, s, and v must be variable. Thus, one or more assumptions of the Harrod-Domar Model must be relaxed. To loosen the rigidity of the Harrod-Domar system, four possible areas of variability may be considered. These involve relaxation of one or more of the following assumptions:

1. Labor demand assumptions.
2. Labor supply assumptions.
3. Technology assumptions.
4. Savings assumptions.

We shall briefly summarize the implications of relaxing the labor market assumptions and, then, focus on relaxing the technology assumptions which involve the capital budgeting criteria. Also, the implications of altering the savings assumptions (which bring the financial mechanism into full play) will be analyzed.

Unemployment Equilibrium Models

This is the class of models closest to static Keynesian theory. The growth rate is determined by demand-side considerations—savings and investment—rather than by the underlying supply-side limitation reflected in the natural rate of growth (n). A high level of s means that the equilibrium rate of growth s/v is high, because only with a high rate of growth will there be enough investment to absorb the high rate of savings; or, the capital output ratio would have to be high to absorb the savings through large investment per unit of output. A low v would call for a high rate of growth for investment to absorb savings. But there is no assurance that a high s or a low v would bring about a high rate of growth necessarily. In addition, unemployment and increasing unemployment would be compatible with the equality of savings and investment. Thus, equilibrium with increasing unemployment might result if s/v is equal to or less than n. When the equilibrium rate of growth is determined from the demand side, a number of models may result. Cyclical fluctuations may be brought into the model as well as ratchet effects.

Flexibility in the Capital Output Ratio

For full employment equilibrium, we must have $n = s/v$ or $v = s/n$. If factors are paid the value of their marginal products, this implies a particular value of real wages, w, and the rate of profit, p. Thus, we can determine what these must be for v to have the desired value.

The solution is indicated by Figure VIII-4.

In Figure VIII-4, R represents a solution for full employment:

$$\frac{1}{v} = \frac{n}{s} \quad \text{and } v = s/n \quad \text{or} \quad n = s/v \quad g_w = s/v$$

Thus, the warranted and natural rates of growth are equal at R. The slope of the tangent $WR = WS/SR$. This measures the marginal productivity of capital, which is $\partial y / \partial k$. Hence, the profit rate, p, at R is determined. The output is divided between profits (WS) and wages (OW).

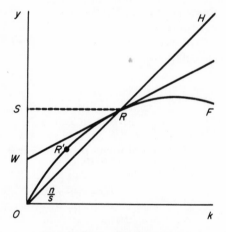

Figure 8-4.   Growth Model

The model has been described as a neo-classical model that provides for equilibrium. It provides for a steady-state relationship between the warranted rate of growth and the natural rate of growth. The natural rate of n is adjusted by the warranted rate of growth, because v is variable. Thus s/v adjusts to n and thus the warranted rate adjusts to the natural rate. Thus, the steady-state rate of growth is independent of s. Given two economies with a different s, but the same n, the economy with the higher s will have a higher v and a higher income per man. But the rate of growth will be the same in the two economies. The rate of growth in each economy will be equal to n, the growth rate in the labor force.

In terms of the Figure VIII-4, equilibrium is achieved by choosing that point on OF so that $s/v = n$, the natural rate of growth. At this point v has adjusted so that $s/v = n$. At that point WR is tangent and determines ρ, the rate of profit which is also the return on capital.

But what is the relevance to financial theory? In order that v gets adjusted, a financial mechanism is required. There must be a rate of interest, r, that leads to investment equal to full-employment savings. Thus, we have brought in both the marginal efficiency of investment function and the savings function. In equilibrium, with no risk, r equals ρ. With risk, ρ is greater than r by the requisite risk premium.

This neo-classical model can accommodate a wide range of investment functions so long as investment is sufficiently interest-elastic to allow the financial mechanism to work. Here again, criteria for capital budgeting decisions are seen to perform an important role. For example, if the cash payback rule is employed, a relatively inelastic investment function is implied. Thus, the constant v of the H-D Model would result. For a full illustration of the important role of the financial mechanism, however, we turn to an analysis of the implications of a varying savings function.

Variants of the Classical Savings Function

The adjustment in s/v can come about through variations in s if v is fixed. While the model could be illustrated for a wide variety of asumptions about the savings function, it can be seen most clearly by exhibiting the extreme case in which the savings-out-of-profits propensity is 1 and the savings-out-of-wages propensity is 0. In this extreme case, we have the following:

$$s\pi = 1 \text{ and } s = \frac{\pi}{Y} \qquad \begin{array}{l} s\pi = \text{propensity to save} \\ \text{by profit receivers} \end{array}$$

In this model, income distribution becomes the adjustment variable. If savings are too high, a shift in income to wage earners whose propensity to save is zero will reduce the over-all savings rate. If the rate of growth is low, because the savings rate is low, a shift in income to profit receivers will increase the over-all savings rate because $s\pi = 1$.

We may now observe the interaction of the variable investment function and the variable savings ratio by considering a growth model in which both a classical savings function and variable capital output ratio obtain. The equation system appears as follows:

$$\frac{\Delta Y}{Y} = \frac{s}{v} = \frac{s\pi\pi}{Y} \cdot \frac{Y}{K} = s\pi \qquad \begin{array}{l} \rho = \pi/K \\ \rho s = s\pi\,(\pi/Y) \end{array}$$

In this model the rate of growth of income must be equal to the rate of growth of capital. The increase in capital is equal to savings, which is equal to profits multiplied by $s\pi$.

The rate of increase of capital is equal to the profit rate multiplied by $s\pi$. The requirement of the natural and warranted rates of growth to be equal becomes $n = s\pi\; \rho$. Since $s\pi = 1$, this relationship reduces to $n = \rho$. In other words, under this assumption of the classical savings function, the profit rate must equal the growth rate. These relationships are exhibited in Figure VIII-5.

In this figure, there is a unique relation between the distribution of income and the amount of capital per man and, hence, v. Full-employment equilibrium at R is achieved if $n = s/v$, the basic steady-state requirement that the natural rate of growth, n, is equal to the warranted rate of growth, s/v. This may be alternatively written $v = sn$. At R, ns equals v since the slope of OF measures the profit rate ρ. The requirement for the equality of the natural and warranted rates of growth is $n = s\pi\; \rho$; this may also be written $n/s\pi = \rho$. At the point R, the slope of the line drawn from W to R is $n/s\pi$. The slope of OF is ρ. Therefore, there is equality between the two at R and, therefore, between the natural rate and the warranted rate of growth. The wage again is OW. The line WR is the warranted rate of growth. It has a different slope from OH in Figure VIII-4 because OH started from the origin and for OH, s differs from $s\pi$. However, in Figure VIII-5, s is equal to $s\pi$. Thus, the line WR starts from W instead of the origin because savings is from non-wage incomes only (SW).

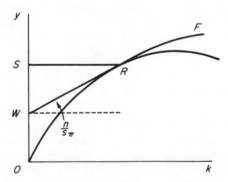

Figure 8-5.   Growth with a Classical Savings Function

The main characteristics of a model in which the savings ratio and the capital output ratio may vary have now been exhibited. But this discussion only begins to indicate the richness of the variety of models that might result. In a sense, the savings ratio and the capital output ratio may be modified and variable in an almost infinite number of ways, and an almost infinite number of resulting growth models can be generated. To illustrate some of the possible models that might result, a few of those that have had a considerable impact on others will be briefly offered.

For example, if the investment function is one in which the desired capital output ratio is a function of the profit rate, the resulting model depends upon the relationship between the profit rate and perhaps a monetarily determined interest rate.[7]

In the Kaldor-Mirrlees model of 1962, the investment and, therefore, the capital output ratio is related to a fixed pay-off period for investment per worker. This reflects the cash payback period among the four main capital budgeting criteria discussed earlier.

Schumpeter's theory of economic growth as summarized by Hahn and Matthews, has an investment function related to profit and a residual type of savings function.[8] All savings is done by business, and they save whatever is needed to finance the investment that has been decided upon on other grounds. The investment rate is a function of P , the profit rate. A steady-state full-employment will be achieved only if P can adjust to the point required to make I/K equal to n because a steady-state full-employment will exist only where I/K equals n. In this model the savings function disappears and only an investment function remains.

The full complexity of the interrelationships is suggested by the following quotation from Hahn and Matthews which ends their section of the discussion of the role of finance in growth models.

> It is plain that a wide variety of treatments of saving are possible. The empirical literature is vast, and research is continuing. With regard to the main issue that has divided writers on growth theory—the issue between the proportional and the classical saving functions—it would be difficult to deny that the proportion of profits saved is greater than the proportion of wages saved, since the propensity to save out of corporate profits is so high. It is tempting therefore to base support of the classical savings function on the institutional characteristics of corporate enterprise without invoking any difference in attitudes between the households that receive profits and households that receive wages. However, it is necessary in this connection to look beyond the mere proportions of corporate and personal income saved. For the addition to the real assets of corporations made possible by corporate savings must affect share values, and in the long run it is difficult to see how share values can diverge widely from the value of real assets. Change in share values is likely to have an influence on the saving behavior of the owners of the shares. In the extreme case where shareholders regard an increase in share values brought about by corporate saving as fully equivalent to the increase in their wealth that would have been brought about by personal saving of an equal amount, a

---

[7] Hahn and Matthews, *op. cit.,* p. 797.
[8] *Ibid.,* p. 797.

given act of corporate saving will lead to a fully equivalent reduction in personal saving below what it would otherwise have been. The retention policies of corporate management will then have no influence on the overall propensity to save of the economy. In that event saving functions of the classical type would have to be based on the supposition of different attitudes on the part of shareholders and wage-earners as persons. This is not the place to pursue these matters.[9]

This long quotation has been reproduced, because it indicates the complexity of the relations and also the potential role of business finance. Dividend policy or retention policy may thus have an important influence on the rate of savings. Since the rate of savings may be a critical variable in the resulting growth model, corporate savings or dividend policies may have a critical role to play in the rate at which the economy grows. Given the importance of growth goals for the American economy, it is clear that business finance has many things of significance to say in this connection. If corporate savings does not affect the over-all savings rate, then the economic processes by which changes in corporate savings rates are adjusted must be clearly understood if public policy is to be consistent with savings rates appropriate for long-run growth goals.

Influence of Financial Factors

The foregoing discussion has relevance for the question of whether financial factors can influence "the real levels of output wages and income" and of the economy as a whole. It is clear that decisions concerning degree of operating leverage a firm employs will affect the scale of operations, the cost structure, and output decisions. The degree of financial leverage employed by the firm will have a parallel impact.

Both investment and financing decisions must be considered. Inherently, the nature of maximizing capital values requires simultaneous and continuous consideration of both investment and financing decisions. As a practical matter, the situation might exist in which the nature of the industry was such that one set of decisions could be made independent of the other set of factors. For example, if the supply of funds were perfectly elastic, then the quantity of investment is dependent solely on the shape and position of the marginal efficiency function. This is what people may have in mind when they say that if the supply of funds is ample, investment decisions are made independent of financing decisions. Investment decisions are made and then financing is obtained. Such a statement of the behavior of the firm is only partially correct. For if the cost of capital function is perfectly elastic and an unlimited amount of funds is available at some market rate, it is still the intersection of the margin efficiency

---

9 Hahn and Matthews, "The Theory of Economic Growth: A Survey," *The Economic Journal*, LXXIV (December, 1964), 800-801.

function with the cost of capital function that determines the amount of investment made by the firm. Conversely, if the marginal efficiency of the investment function is perfectly inelastic, the amount of investment is determined solely by the position of the marginal efficiency of investment function. The cost of capital is relevant only for influencing the equilibrium rate of interest.

Still another possibility is that the intersection of the marginal efficiency function with the cost of capital function occurs in a perfectly inelastic segment of the cost of capital function. In this case the shape and position of the marginal efficiency of investment function has no influence on the amount of investment that will take place. The shape and position of the marginal efficiency investment function will again determine only the equilibrium rate of interest. But the shape and position of either the marginal efficiency of investment function or the cost of capital function are matters for empirical determination. It is not necessary to take a position on what the empirical facts are with reference to the nature of the marginal efficiency of investment function or to the cost of capital function for the firm. But clearly the nature of these two functions and their equilibrium relationships have great significance for the operations of the firm and for the behavior of the economy as a whole.

The financial mechanism is important both for the investment decisions and the cost of capital conditions of the individual firm. Aggregated, these determine the position and shape of the investment function and the savings function for the economy as a whole. The business finance area provides insights on these influences. It is in the business finance area that recognition is given to liquidity needs of the firm, the need to balance debt leverage in relationship to prospective growth and stability of sales and income, and the recognition of the asset and financing decisions of the firm as types of portfolio decisions. The influence of uncertainty can be observed in the financial decisions with respect to liquidity, leverage, and portfolio balance. The decisions of financial managers, thus, have import beyond the management of the individual enterprises.

References

Ackoff, Russell L. and Patrick Rivett, *A Manager's Guide to Operations Research*. New York: John Wiley & Sons, Inc., 1963, Chap. 2.

Alchian, Armen, "Costs and Outputs," *The Allocation of Economic Resources*. Stanford, Cal.: Stanford University Press, 1959.

American Management Association, Inc., *The Financial Executive's Job*. New York: The Association, 1952.

———, *New Responsibilities in Corporate Finance,* Report No. 71. New York: The Association, 1962.

———, *The Financial Manager's Job*. New York: The Association, 1963.

Baumes, Carl G., *Division Financial Executives,* Studies in Business Policy No. 101. New York: National Industrial Conference Board, Inc., 1961.

Bendix, R., "Bureaucratization in Industry," *Industrial Conflict*. New York: McGraw-Hill Book Company, 1954, Chap. 12.

Beranek, William, *The Effect of Leverage on the Market Value of Common Stock*. Madison, Wis.: Bureau of Business Research and Service, University of Wisconsin, 1965.

Berle, A. A. Jr., and G. C. Means, *The Modern Corporation and Private Property*. New York: The Macmillan Company, 1944, pp. 119-25.

Bierman, Harold, Jr., "Probability, Statistical Decision Theory and Accounting," *The Accounting Review,* XXXVII (July, 1962), 400-405.

Bosland, Chelcie C., *Corporate Finance and Regulation*. New York: The Ronald Press Company, 1949.

———, "Materials and Methods of Teaching Business Finance (IV)," *Journal of Finance,* V (September, 1950), pp. 287-88.

Boulding, Kenneth E., *A Reconstruction of Economics*. New York: John Wiley & Sons, Inc., 1950.

Bradshaw, T. F., "The Place and Status of the Financial Executive Today," Financial Management Series, No. 99. New York: American Management Association, Inc. ,1952, pp. 14-22.

Brewer, D. E. and J. B. Michaelsen, "The Cost of Capital, Corporation Finance, and the Theory of Investment: Comment," *The American Economic Review*, LV (June, 1965), 516-23.

Brown, Alvin, *Financial Approach to Industrial Operations*. New York: Society for the Advancement of Management, 1957, p. 7.

Sprague, Lucy Mitchell, "A Personal Sketch," *Wesley Clair Mitchell, The Economic Scientist*, Arthur F. Burns (ed.). New York: National Bureau of Economic Research, Inc., 1952, pp. 94-95.

Calkins, Francis J., "Materials and Methods of Teaching Business Finance (II)," *Journal of Finance*, V (September, 1950), 276.

Capon, Frank S., "Financial Management in the 70's," *Financial Executive*, October, 1963, pp. 24-29.

Clarkson, G. P. E., *Portfolio Selection: A Simulation of Trust Investment*. Englewood Cliffs, N.J.: Prentice-Hall, Inc., 1962.

Coase, R. H., "The Nature of the Firm," *Economica*, IV (November, 1937), 386-405.

Cooper, W. W., "Theory of the Firm: Some Suggestions for Revision," *The American Economic Review*, XXXIX (December, 1949), 1205-07.

Curtis, Edward T., *Company Organization of the Finance Function, American Management Association*, Research Study No. 55. New York: The Association, Inc., 1962.

Cyert, Richard M. and James G. March, *A Behavioral Theory of the Firm*. Englewood Cliffs, N.J.: Prentice-Hall, Inc., 1963.

Dauten, Carl A., "Toward a Theory of Business Finance: The Necessary Ingredients of a Theory of Business Finance," *The Journal of Finance*, X (May, 1955), 107.

Dean, Joel, *Capital Budgeting*. New York: Columbia University Press, 1951.

Dean, Neal J., "Looking Ahead: New Developments, New Tools," *The Financial Manager's Job*. New York: American Management Association, Inc., 1957, pp. 443-44.

Dewing, Arthur Stone, *Corporate Promotions and Reorganizations*. Cambridge, Mass.: Harvard University Press, 1930.

————, *The Financial Policy of Corporations*. New York: The Ronald Press Company, 1943.

Donaldson, Gordon, "Financial Goals; Management vs. Stockholders," *Harvard Business Review*, May-June, 1963, 110.

————, "Looking Around—Finance for the Nonfinancial," *Harvard Business Review*, XXXVIII, No. 1 January-February 1960, 33-36 ff.

Dougall, Herbert E., *Capital Markets and Institutions*. Englewood Cliffs, N.J.: Prentice-Hall, Inc., 1965.

"The Egghead Millionaires," in *Financial Management: New Challenges and Responsibilities*, J. F. Weston (ed.). New York: Holt, Rinehart & Winston, Inc., 1965.

"Meet NIG's Chief Financial Officer," *Finance*, March 15, 1961, pp. 35-36.

"Meet the Treasurer of Philip Morris, Inc.," *Finance*, March 15, 1961, pp. 45-47.

Fisher, Irving, *The Theory of Interest*. New York: The Macmillan Company, 1930.

Flemming, J. S. and Feldstein, M. S., "Present Value versus Internal Rate of Return: A Comment," *Economic Journal*, LXXIV, No. 294 (June, 1964), 490-91.

"The New Power of the Financial Executives," *Fortune*, LXV (January, 1962), 81-85, 138-43.

Gold, Bela and Ralph M. Kraus, "Integrating Physical with Financial Measures for Managerial Controls," *Academy of Management Journal*, VII (June, 1964), 109-27.

Gordon, Myron J., *The Investment, Financing and Valuation of the Corporation*. Homewood, Ill.: Richard D. Irwin, Inc., 1962.

———, "Security and a Financial Theory of Investment," *The Quarterly Journal of Economics*, LXXIV (August, 1960), 472.

Gordon, R. A., *Business Leadership in the Large Corporation*. Washington, D.C.: The Brookings Institution, 1945.

———, *Quarterly Journal of Economics*, L (1935-36), 622-57; LII (1937-38), 367-400; LIV (1939-40), 455-73.

Grayson, C. Jackson Jr., "Introduction of Uncertainty into Capital Budgeting Decisions," *NAA Bulletin*, XLIII (January, 1962), 79-80.

Griswold, John, *Cash Flow Through a Business*. Hanover, N.H.: Amos Tuck School of Business Administration, Dartmouth College, 1955.

Guthmann, H. and H. Dougall, *Corporate Financial Policy*. Englewood Cliffs, N.J.: Prentice-Hall, Inc., 1940, p. 1.

Halley, D. M., "Materials and Methods of Teaching Business Finance (I)," *Journal of Finance*, V (September, 1950), 273.

Harris, William B., "RCA Organizes for Profit," *Fortune* (August, 1957), pp. 110-15.

Herzog, John P., "Investor Experience in Corporate Securities: A New Technique for Measurement," *The Journal of Finance*, XIX (March, 1964), 46-62.

Hirschleifer, Jack, "On the Theory of Optimal Investment Decision," *Journal of Political Economy*, LXVI (August, 1958), 329-52.

———, "The Firm's Cost Function: A Successful Reconstruction?," *Journal of Business*, XXXV (July, 1962), 235-55.

Howard, Bion B., and Upton, Miller, *Introduction to Business Finance*. New York: McGraw-Hill Book Company, 1953.

Hunt, Pearson, "Financial Policy of Corporations," *Quarterly Journal of Economics*, February, 1943, pp. 303-13.

————, "Materials and Methods of Teaching Business Finance (III)," *Journal of Finance,* V (September, 1950), 284.

Jackson, H. H., *The Controller: His Functions and Organization.* Cambridge, Mass.: Harvard University Press, 1948.

Jerrett, Robert Jr., "Integrating and Coordinating the Treasury and Controllership Functions," *The Financial Manager's Job.* New York: American Management Association, Inc., 1957, pp. 37-38.

Joseph, Seeber, and Bach, Economic Analysis and Policy: Background Readings for Current Issues. Englewood Cliffs, N.J.: Prentice-Hall, Inc., 1966.

Ketchum, Marshall D., "Looking Around," *Harvard Business Review,* XXXIV, No. 1 (January-February, 1956), 132.

Koopmans, Tjalling C., "Measurement Without Theory," *The Review of Economics and Statistics,* XXIX (August, 1947), 161-72.

Kuznets, Simon, *Capital in the American Economy—Its Formation and Financing.* Princeton, N.J.: Princeton University Press, 1961.

Lewis, Ben W., "The Corporate Entrepreneur," *Quarterly Journal of Economics,* LI (May, 1937), 534-44.

Lincoln, Freeman, "John Mecom's Delightful Dilemma," *Fortune* (June, 1957), pp. 169-72, 249-60.

————, "Big Wheeler-Dealer from Dallas," *Fortune* (February, 1953), pp. 152-54, 226-37.

Lintner, John, "Optimal Dividends and Corporate Growth Under Uncertainty," *The Quarterly Journal of Economics,* LXXVIII (February, 1964), 49-95.

Margolis, Julius, "The Analysis of the Firm: Rationalism, Conventionalism, and Behaviorism," *Journal of Business,* XXXI (July, 1958), 187-99.

Marris, Robin, *The Economic Theory of "Managerial" Capitalism.* New York: Free Press of Glencoe, Inc., 1964.

Marting, Elizabeth and Robert E. Finley (eds.), *The Financial Manager's Job.* New York: American Management Association, Inc., 1964.

McKinsey, J. O., and Stuart Meech, *Controlling the Finances of a Business.* New York: The Ronald Press Company, 1923.

Meiselman, David and Eli Shapiro, *The Measurement of Corporate Sources and Uses of Funds.* New York: National Bureau of Economic Research, 1964.

Modigliani, Franco and Merton H. Miller, "The Cost of Capital, Corporation Finance and the Theory of Investments," *The American Economic Review,* June, 1958, 261-96.

Moller, George, "The Financial Executive in Over-all Company Planning," *The Controller,* XXX (January, 1962), 17.

National Industrial Conference Board, Inc., *Military Inspection in Industry.* ("Studies in Business Policy," No. 50.) New York: The Board, 1951.

National Industrial Conference Board, Inc., *The Duties of Financial Executives.* ("Studies in Business Policy," No. 56.) New York: The Board, 1952.

"The New Power of the Financial Executive," in *Financial Management in the 1960's: New Challenges and Responsibilities,* J. F. Weston (ed.). New York: Holt, Rinehart & Winston, Inc., 1965.

Penrose, Edith Tilton, *The Theory of the Growth of the Firm.* New York: John Wiley & Sons, Inc., 1959, pp. 218-20.

Peterson, H. G., "The Co-ordination of Company Financial Planning with External Economic Conditions," *National Association of Cost Accountants Bulletin,* XXVII (March, 1946), 575-87.

Pettit, L. E., "Investor Relations: New Challenge to Management," *American Management Association, Management Report, No. 71.* New York: The Association, 1962, p. 67.

Pflomm, Norman E., *Managing Company Cash,* Studies in Business Policy No. 99. New York: National Industrial Conference Board, Inc., 1961.

———, *Financial Committees,* Studies in Business Policy No. 105. New York: National Industrial Conference Board, Inc., 1962.

Plummer, G. F., "The Financial Executive: His Role in the Corporate Organization," *Controller,* XXX (January, 1962), 16 ff.

Porterfield, James T. S., *Investment Decisions and Capital Costs.* Englewood Cliffs, N.J.: Prentice-Hall, Inc., 1965.

Samuelson, Paul A., *Economics: An Introductory Analysis.* New York: McGraw-Hill Book Company, Inc., 1961, p. 647.

Schiff, Michael and Martin Mellman, *Financial Management of the Marketing Function.* New York: Financial Executives Research Foundation, Inc., 1962.

Shubik, Martin, "Approaches to the Study of Decision-Making Relevant to the Firm," *Journal of Business,* XXXIV (April, 1961), 101-18.

Simon, Herbert A., "Organizing for Controllership: Centralizing and Decentralization," *Controller,* January, 1955, p. 13.

———, "Theories of Decision-Making in Economics," *American Economic Review,* XLIX (June, 1959), 253-83.

Sloan, Alfred P. Jr., *My Years with General Motors.* New York: Doubleday and Company, Inc., 1964.

Soldofsky, Robert M., "Accountant's vs. Economist's Concepts of Break-Even Analysis," *National Association of Accountants Bulletin,* December, 1959, pp. 5-18.

Solomon, Ezra, *The Management of Corporate Capital.* Chicago, Ill.: Graduate School of Business, University of Chicago, 1959.

———, *The Theory of Financial Management.* New York: Columbia University Press, 1963.

Stedry, Andrew C., *Budget Control and Cost Behavior.* Englewood Cliffs, N.J.: Prentice-Hall, Inc., 1960.

Steiner, George A., *Managerial Long Range Planning.* New York: McGraw-Hill Book Company, 1963.

Stryker, Perrin, "P & C for Profit," *Fortune* (April, 1952), 128-29, 156-62.

Thompson, Stewart, *How Companies Plan,* American Management Association Research Study No. 54. New York: The Association, Inc., 1962.

Turvey, R., "Present Value versus Internal Rate of Return—An Essay in the Theory of the Third Best," *Economic Journal,* LXXIII, No. 289 (March, 1963), 93-98.

Van Arsdall, Paul, "Discussion: Toward a Theory of Business Finance," *Journal of Finance,* X (May, 1955), 146.

Vance, Jack O., "The Changing Role of the Corporate Financial Executive," *Financial Executive,* XXXI, No. 3 (March, 1963), 27-29.

Weston, J. Fred., "A Test of Cost of Capital Propositions," *The Southern Economics Journal,* XXX (October, 1963), 105-12.

————, "The Finance Function," *Journal of Finance,* IX (September, 1954), 265-82.

————, *Managerial Finance.* New York: Holt, Rinehart & Winston, Inc., 1962.

————, *The Role of Mergers in the Growth of Large Firms.* Berkeley, Calif.: University of California Press, 1953, pp. 31-32.

————, *Financial Management in the 1960's: New Challenges and Responsibilities.* New York: Holt, Rinehart & Winston, Inc., 1966.

Wilder, Raymond L., *Introduction to the Foundations of Mathematics.* New York: John Wiley & Sons, Inc., 1952, pp. 3-49.

Williams, Charles M., "Discussion: Toward a Theory of Business Finance," *Journal of Finance,* X (May, 1955), 150.

Index